Unique Selling Propositions in Tourism

Research Insights from the Caribbean Region

Babu P George, PhD, DBA

Summary

The 'unique selling proposition' (USP) is a marketing idea that gained popularity among both academicians and practitioners, at least since the 1950's. Marketers knew for long that it is not enough to differentiate; equally important it is to *propositionalize* the basis of differentiation. The television advertising guru Rosser Reeves called for advertisements to be reflective of this and coined the term USP. Since then, marketing based on the USP concept has become ever popular. Just like various other industries, various tourism destination promotional campaigns began to highlight USPs that make these destinations distinct and different. However, scholarly investigations about the development or management of these campaigns remained very limited.

This mixed methods research examines the dynamics of implementation of the USP based marketing among the Caribbean tourism destination countries. In particular, it compares the extent of USP adoption in the web-based marketing campaigns of these countries over a timeline from 2004 to 2014. Data gathered by the researcher for 2004, 2009, and 2014, indicates that there has been an increase in the use of unique selling propositions during 2004-2009; however, by 2014, many countries have reduced the use of USPs in their promotional campaigns. Also, over the years, destinations high in attraction diversity tended to delimit themselves from using highly targeted unique selling propositions while their counterparts with less attraction diversity routinely employed hierarchically superior USP slogans. The exact number of attractions in a destination country did not significantly imply the choice of slogans as much as the attraction type diversity. Attraction diversity is found to moderate the relationship between the level of USP used and tourist arrivals. A theme that emerged from the qualitative interviews was that

USP statements in attraction diverse destinations tended to result in greater gaps between tourist expectations and their actual experience. In order to achieve the objectives of this study, the present researcher developed an 'attraction diversity index', which is conceived to be a measure of the diversity of attraction types in a destination area. The research also discusses the relative power of stakeholders representing different attraction clusters and how this power dynamic might determine the final choice of national tourism slogans.

Table of Contents

List of Figures

List of Tables

List of Abbreviations

AMA   American Marketing Association

ACE   Attraction Cluster Equity

ADI   Attraction Diversity Index

CTO   Caribbean Tourism Organization

DMO   Destination Marketing Organization

HHI   Herfindahl-Hirschman Index

IBM   International Business Machine

PASW   Predictive Analytics Software

SPSS   Statistical Package for Social Sciences

U.S.   United States of America

USP   Unique Selling Proposition

USVI   United States Virgin Islands

WTO   World Tourism Organization

WTTC   World Travel and Tourism Council

List of Appendices

Chapter 1: Overview

Since early 2000's, the Sun-Sea-Sand-Sex model of tourism in the Caribbean began to face significant challenges (Henthorne, George, & Smith, 2013; Weiler & Dehoorne, 2014). In fact, a few destination countries in the Caribbean anticipated this and began searching for competitive advantage elsewhere (de Holan & Phillips, 1997). Authors like Poon (1998) and Henthorne & Miller (2003) urged that the only way the Caribbean can sustain its tourism in the 21st century is by means of innovations in products and processes. These searches, however, did not result in the identification of any radically innovative products and the workable alternative for most of these destinations was to concoct some kind of uniqueness in the commonness (Mosedale, 2006). For many destinations, this meant interpreting and reinterpreting the value of tourism resources until that process resulted in the identification of something unique (Chambers & McIntosh, 2008). Based on such sought and found ideas, these destinations unleased various promotional campaigns (Croes, 2006). The ideas developed, thus, were expected to be the Unique Selling Propositions (USP)s of these designations.

Taking forward the pioneering effort by Henthorne & Miller (2003) and Miller & Henthorne (2006), the present research critically examines the USP based tourism marketing campaigns of the Caribbean island destinations during 2004-2014 and identifies certain key issues that are relevant for both marketing theory and practice. In other words, this mixed methods research is a return to the Caribbean, for an updated and expanded examination of USP-based tourism campaigns by the same destinations.

Based on longitudinal data analysis, higher level USP use was found to initially rise, reach a peak, and then decline. In order to better understand how the diversity of attractions in a destination management area influences USP adoption decisions, the researcher proposed and developed a methodological tool: attraction diversity index. It was observed that, over the years, destinations high in attraction diversity tended to delimit themselves from using highly targeted USPs while their counterparts with less attraction diversity routinely employed hierarchically superior USP slogans. The exact number of attractions did not significantly imply the choice of slogans as much as attraction diversity. Attraction diversity significantly reduced the impact of USP usage upon tourist arrivals. The relative political power of stakeholders representing different attraction clusters and how this power dynamic might determine the choice of the national tourism organization's USP slogan also are also included in the scope of this research.

Background

Caribbean tourist destinations are increasingly realizing the need to fight together for the tourist. The Caribbean Tourism Organization (CTO) has been encouraging member nations to identify elements that make each of them unique so that marketing dollars are not wasted in competing against one another (Hill, & Lewis, 2015). Still, for the mass tourist, the Caribbean is still a single, largely indistinguishable, region. The geography and climate in the Caribbean region does vary, but not so much distinguishable to the gaze of the touristic eyes. National destination management organizations and tourism industry bodies of each country in the Caribbean have struggled hard to differentiate their country from all others, but again with not so much success (Croes, 2006).

Miller & Henthorne (2006) examined the ways the Caribbean destinations distinguish themselves from their competitors in terms of distinctive attractions, strategies, price levels, culture, history, landscape, music, cuisine, and other attributes. That study brought the USP concept from the generic marketing literature to an international tourism context, while also updating the analysis to the 21st century Web-based marketing technology. Miller and

Henthorne argued for the appropriateness of the USP concept in international tourism in general, and the Caribbean as a study region in particular:

> The intense competitiveness of the global tourism industry increasingly demands of destinations the most effective possible marketing, including product development, image creation, and promotional strategy. This necessity is nowhere more evident than for the Caribbean region: itself a highly fractured and intra-competitive collection of small destinations, which also must compete with a world of increasingly aggressive and expanding tourism alternatives (Miller & Henthorne, 2006, p. 49).

The analysis by Miller & Henthorne (2006) concluded that the marketing campaigns of the Caribbean countries could be classified in a meaningful and useful manner following the USP hierarchy. On the other hand, it was also observed that tourism marketing based on the USP was rarely implemented in its true spirit, even more than four decades past the concept's introduction.

The Research Problem

Despite differences in the specifics, marketing literature is in general agreement that identifying some kinds of uniqueness is a crucial element of the marketing process; especially, it is essential for successful positioning with a meaningful difference (Frazer, 1983; Kippenberger, 2000; Laskey, Fox & Crask, 1995; Schlegelmilch, 2016). Unique selling ideas over periods of refinement could transform into the core competency of a business (Knox & Bickerton, 2003). However, the adoption of USPs is tourism is not as straightforward as it is in most other industries. Tourism is a highly subjective, interpretative, and experiential product; it does not have an obvious core, to which the experiences of all customers could be anchored. Success stories of the USP approach are nonetheless rare (Deslandes & Goldsmith, 2015).

Given the various and significant benefits and costs associated with the use of the USP based tourism marketing approach (Blain, Levy, & Ritchie, 2005; Deslandes & Goldsmith, 2015; Shanka, 2001), the primary research question to be addressed is whether, as the Caribbean country destinations continue to evolve and mature, the historical trend towards the increasing use of the USP approach will sustain. An associated question is whether small and less diverse destination countries are more likely to adopt USP based tourism marketing campaigns than their larger and more diverse counterparts. This appears likely given large countries with diverse attractions may have more diverse interest groups, thus making USP choices and their adoption problematic (Daye, 2010). This author also felt that the branding strategies of the Carribbean countries she chose for study were gravely undifferentiated in both functional and symbolic brand image appeals.

Qualitative reviews of Caribbean tourism literature and informal interviews with the various stakeholders conducted by the present researcher led to the belief that, in destination countries with high attraction diversity, there may be substantially more industry resistance to adopting a USP approach. Stated another way, in large and diverse tourism destination countries, slogans representing the USP will be delimited to the lower levels of a hierarchy of slogans. Also, businesses that traditionally marketed attractions not in conformity to their destinations' official USP campaigns might tend to realign their products and services to reflect better match. Finally, based on the Caribbean cruise arrival data about Jamaica (CTO, 2014), the researcher proposed to investigate whether the USP of the island destination or its attraction diversity could inform tourists' vacation choice.

Research Questions

This research proposed to address the following questions:

RQ1   As the Caribbean country destinations continue to evolve and mature, is there still a continuing trend toward the increasing use of the USP approach?

RQ2   What is the relationship between the attraction diversity of a destination management area and the level of USP usage in that destination area's promotional campaigns?

RQ3   Does a destination's attraction diversity significantly moderate the relationship between the USP usage and tourist arrivals?

RQ4   How do businesses differentiate themselves within the homogeneity implied by their destination's USP statement?

Research Question 4 was addressed exploratively and qualitatively. The remaining questions were subjected to statistical confirmation based on primary survey data or secondary data derived from public records. The findings were contrasted with additional qualitative observations and informal feedback from the practitioners.

Hypotheses

The hypotheses related to questions 1, 2, and 3 are stated below:

Null hypothesis H1.0: There is no significant difference in the levels of unique selling propositions used by the Caribbean nations in their marketing programs, across the period of study i.e., 2004-2014.

Alternate Hypothesis H1.1: There has been a significant increase in the levels of unique selling propositions used by the Caribbean nations in their marketing programs, across the period of study i.e., 20 04-2014.

Null hypothesis H2.0: There is no significant relationship between the attraction diversity of a destination area and the level of USP usage in that destination area's promotional campaigns.

Alternate Hypothesis H2.1: There is a significant inverse relationship between the attraction diversity of a destination area and the level of USP usage in that destination area's promotional campaigns.

Null hypothesis H3.0: Attraction diversity of a destination area does not significantly moderate the relationship between the level of unique selling proposition used and tourist arrivals.

Alternate Hypothesis H3.1: The relationship between the level of unique selling proposition used and tourist arrivals is significantly moderated by the attraction diversity of a destination area.

A critical impediment in the current literature on tourism marketing is the absence of a methodology and a tool to quantify and measure attraction diversity. Hence, in order to answer the research questions, the researcher first attempted to develop a methodological tool to measure attraction diversity. The tool developed, fashioned after the Herfindahl-Hirschman Index (HHI), is named "Attraction Diversity Index (ADI)" and its inverse is named "Attraction Cluster Equity (ACE)". The ACE concept is postulated to be a valid measure of attraction concentration a.k.a. monopoly of particular attraction types in a destination area.

From the analysis of data, the historical trend of increasing use of USPs evinced during the early stages of USP based campaigns has peaked and has given way to more differentiated uses, reflecting attraction diversity and the politically charged power dynamics in destinations. In particular, the researcher noticed significant inverse relationship between a destination management area's attraction diversity and the level of USP that it uses in its promotional campaigns. Finally, findings indicate that ADI moderates the relationship between USP level and tourist arrivals.

Summary

Based on 2004 data (CTO, 2004), most Caribbean destinations competed head-on against one another in their Web-based marketing campaigns, based on similar and highly generic slogans and imagery. Standard beach images predominated, along with "one-size-fits-all" slogans such as Anguilla's "Tranquility Wrapped in Blue." Destinations with non-unique selling propositions then included several of the region's major tourism players: Bermuda, Cuba, Puerto Rico, the Bahamas, Jamaica, the Dominican Republic. At the same time, however, a few highly creative campaigns demonstrated the potential for inventing truly noteworthy USPs for tourism destinations – and implementing these USP-based campaigns on the web (Miller & Henthorne, 2007).

These creative websites included some of the smallest players in the region, such as:

Dominica: "The nature island of the Caribbean"

Suriname: "The Beating Heart of the Amazon"

Jamaica: "Get All Right"

Anguilla: "Tranquility wrapped in blue"

Antigua: "The beach is just the beginning"

Aruba: "One happy island"

Barbados: "Long live life"

British Virgin Islands: "nature's little secrets"

Cayman Islands: "Wherever you find your smile, you'll find ours"

Curacao: "Unique Caribbean island paradise"

Dominican Island: "Has it all!"

Grenada: "The spice of the Caribbean"

Haiti: "experience it"

Martinique: "The flower of the Caribbean"

Web-based marketing, in its infancy at the time, opened up a more level playing field among the big-budget and small-budget destinations, and might reward the more creative campaigns that made use of uniquely compelling images and slogans. As the analysis from this research and presented in this thesis would show, the USP approach was found to be quite rewarding until the middle of the study period. Then, it began to show a decline. In the present study, the researcher inquired further into this and various related issues in tourism marketing, in the context of the Caribbean.

The rest of this thesis document is structured as follows: Chapter 2 presents relevant literature for the study; Chapter 3 describes the research methodology chosen; Chapter 4 details the analytical procedures applied upon the data gathered for the study and the findings; and, Chapter 5 offers conclusions of the study, including directions for future researchers.

Chapter 2: Situating the Study in the Literature

In Chapter 2, a summary of the literature reviewed for this study is presented. It will offer an overview of tourism in the Caribbean, highlighting its past, present, and future. Tourism development in the small Caribbean countries is nuanced and is riddled with challenges. The struggles of development will be discussed, with special reference to the Caribbean context. Followed by this, the idea of USP and its implementation in the Caribbean tourism is presented. In its basic form, unique selling propositions are used to articulate the expected intangible experiences associated with destination visits. In particular, cooperative branding is discussed: smaller among the Caribbean islands find merit in this approach because it helps them fend of competitive pressures from their larger neighbors. Finally, the concept of "attraction diversity" is introduced. Attraction diversity is argued to determine the effectiveness of the unique selling proposition based marketing approach.

Tourism in the Caribbean Region

The Caribbean region consists of the Caribbean Sea, its islands, and the surrounding coasts (Mintz, 1983). The region lies southeast of the Gulf of Mexico and the North American mainland, east of Central America, and north of South America. The region has more than 700 islands and numerous other small land-forms like islets, reefs, and cays and is a sub-system of the still wider West Indies region. The term "Caribbean countries" does not have a specific geographical boundary; it depends upon the perspective of the observer (Conway, 1998). According to a generally agreed notion, the countries in the Caribbean include: Anguilla, Antigua and Barbuda, Aruba, Bahamas, Barbados, British Virgin Islands, Cayman Islands, Cuba, Dominica, Dominican Republic, Grenada, Guadeloupe, Haiti, Jamaica, Martinique, Montserrat, Netherlands Antilles, Puerto Rico, Saint Barthelemy, Saint Kitts & Nevis, Saint Lucia, Saint

Martin, Saint Vincent, Trinidad & Tobago, Turks & Caicos Islands, and US Virgin Islands

("Caribbean", n.d.). The geo-political map of the Caribbean region is provided in Figure 1.

Since the mid-20th century, tropical islands worldwide began to move from colonial

export staples to coveted tourism destinations for conspicuous consumption and the Caribbean

region took the lead in this regard (Barker, 1998). The Caribbean region constitutes relatively

homogeneous microstates similar in size, socio-cultural history, and natural forms, which led to

the emphasis of mass production of touristic experiences. No surprise that mass tourism products

for the cruising tourists became the main economic activity of these island nations.

Figure 1. Map of the Caribbean region

The mass tourism orientation built around scarce resources meant high degrees of

environmental exploitation and degradation; an unsustainable stress upon short term prospects at

the expense of inter-generational equity (Parry, Sherlock, & Maingot, 1987). Tourism

penetration index in small Caribbean islands is significantly much higher than that in typical

countries of similar dimensions, observed McElroy and De Albuquerque (1998). Mass customization is probably an alternative (Piore & Sable, 1984). However, Poon (1990) argued that Caribbean islands are not ideally suited for flexible specialization in the tourism industry.

The Caribbean as a Cruising Paradise

Many islands in the Caribbean are small, with low population and very scarce natural resources for production: given their 'exotic' locations and their closeness to the affluent North America, cruise tourism has become for them a natural choice for economic development (McElroy & De Albuquerque, 1998). Their dependence on cruise tourism dollars is so deeply entrenched, often times ecological and aesthetic carrying capacities are exceeded but policy makers consider them as 'normal' (Griffin, 2016). According to Wood (2000), Caribbean tourism can be viewed as a microcosm of globalization at sea. This, however, only complicates the analysis of Caribbean tourism. The deep economic dependency of the Caribbean region on tourism, the inequity of power relations between the various stakeholder groups, and the lack of proven collaboration within this fragmented region of culturally diverse islands are issues that have to be considered in any meaningful analysis of tourism in the Caribbean (Henthorne & George, 2009; Lester & Weeden, 2004).

Despite Europe and Asia-Pacific gaining in importance on the cruise tourism map, the demand for cruise tourism has been mostly from the United States. Caribbean tourism has always remained the first of its beneficiaries. Wilkinson (1999) observed, until the beginning of 21st century, Caribbean cruise tourism suffered from poor planning and haphazard policy interventions due to the lack of sufficient information support for decision makers. Wilkinson voiced that the available statistics were utmost elementary. Issues like deficient and unreliable tourism data focusing on simplistic measures gathered over a short time-span, questionable analysis at a superficial level, unrealistic predictions based on these data, faulty assumptions, and so on, were identified to substantiate his point of view. Yet, in terms of numbers, the development of cruise tourism in the Caribbean over the past two decades has been unparalleled. Each year over one million cruise travelers visit Jamaica to experience a quick sampling of its resort centers such as Montego Bay, Ocho Rios, Negril, Port Antonio, and the growing South Coast.

Since most cruise tourists typically spend only less than a day at each port of call, accommodation revenue from them is very limited. The major source of revenue from cruise tourists is from shopping; most cruise tourists spend a significant amount of time in shopping. Shopping is considered good for the local economy since most shop owners are small scale local businessmen. Even though cruise tourists do not stay overnight, many of them visit local restaurants to taste the local cuisines, which also benefits the local community at large. The island authorities also collect a significant amount from cruise liners for docking ships in the ports (Henthorne, George, & Smith, 2013).

Of late, the industry has been quite proactive in supporting cruise tourism infrastructure development in the Caribbean. For example, The Port Authority of Jamaica and Royal Caribbean Cruise Lines, under a joint venture agreement, began constructing a modern cruise facility in Falmouth, the only one of its kind in Jamaica that can accommodate the new Genesis Class cruise vessels (CTO, 2009). Every year, new destinations, ports, and itineraries are added to the Caribbean cruise tourism product mix. Among other things, this development also is expected to increase the propensity for repeat purchase. Often implied in the industry circles is that the USP of the Caribbean is "being friendly to cruise tourists".

The Concept of the Unique Selling Proposition

The concept of the unique selling proposition and its application to advertising is generally credited to Reeves (1961). The purchasers of unique products will obtain specific unique benefits from consuming those particular products (Bao & Shao 2002). Richardson and Cohen operationalized and tested the USP concept in their 1993 comparative study of tourism marketing campaigns for the United States (U.S.). Richardson and Cohen developed a hierarchical scale for analyzing states' marketing slogans, which ranged from "Level 0: No proposition" through "Level 4b: Unique selling proposition" (p. 95).

Richardson and Cohen (1993) identified four primary criteria in the use of the USP approach to advertising. First, the advertisement must make specific claims substantial enough to be either considered true or false by consumers. Second, the advertisement should forward only one distinct proposition. Third, the advertisement describes what specific benefits are to be realized through the consumption of the product. Fourth, the consumer benefits have to be unique to the advertised product. In essence, a product's USP communicates what is unique about the brand and what sets it apart from the competition.

Richardson and Cohen (1993) created the following hierarchical categorization of marketing slogans, for their analysis of tourism campaigns by U.S. states:

- Level 0: No proposition
- Level 1: Proposition equivalent to "Buy our product"
- Level 2: Proposition equivalent to "Our product is good"
- Level 3a: Proposition gives a product attribute, but virtually any [tourism destination] could claim the same attribute

- Level 3b: Proposition gives a product attribute, but many [tourism destinations] claim the same attribute

- Level 4a: Proposition gives a unique product attribute which is not a product benefit (i.e., does not "sell")

- Level 4b: Unique selling proposition (Richardson and Cohen 1993, p. 95).

A uniquely competitive USP must also display to consumers: (a) an eagerness to sell the product; (b) the desirability of the product to the potential customer; and (c) an assertion the product is not just special but truly unique. In essence, the marketer is seeking to create a uniquely positive brand image – ideally, a brand image that can be captured in a single memorable slogan (e.g., "What happens in Vegas, stays in Vegas").

When M&M advertises "*The milk chocolate melts in your mouth, not in your hand*", when FedEx promises "*When it absolutely, positively has to be there overnight*", or when DeBeers assures "*A diamond is forever*", each of these companies is inviting customers with a unique proposition. An effective slogan should deliver a strong message about the USP to the market (Reeves 1961). While originally proposed as pertaining to product marketing, the USP concept has been extended to encompass services (Chiagouris 2005; Linning 2004) and destinations (Miller & Henthorne 2006; Plog 2004; Richardson & Cohen 1993).

USP Oriented Branding

To be effective, an advertisement should capture attention, awaken interest, and arouse a desire to purchase the promoted product (Echtner & Ritchie 1993). The USP has been considered a critical component in this effectiveness (Warner 2004) and is an integral component in modern-day branding efforts (Lee, Cai, & O'Leary 2005). In destination marketing, successful branding efforts are designed to differentiate a destination from other competitive destinations and to develop for that destination a unique personality in the marketplace (Morgan, Pritchard, & Pride 2004; Prebensen 2007). Branding is viewed as being particularly important for high value, infrequently purchased and highly differentiated items (e.g., destinations) (Rowley 2004). One component central to the destination branding process is a strong destination image (Aaker 1991; Baloglu, Henthorne & Sahin 2014; Echtner & Richie 1993).

Aaker and Joachimsthaler (2000) went on to state that a well-differentiated and consistent image is a necessity in successful branding strategies today. Destination branding has been shown to be a tool that can be used to gain a competitive advantage over other similar destinations (Murphy, Benckendorff, & Moscardo 2007). Conversely, Daye (2010) showed the muddled results that may result from undifferentiated destination brand images. In any case, USPs and the slogans designed to capture them are central to many destinations' branding efforts.

A remarkable destination image has been well established to impact destination selection (Baloglu 1999; Gartner 1996), therefore, if a destination is to remain competitive in the ever-crowded marketplace, a "unique identity" is more important than ever (Morgan, Pritchard, & Piggott 2003). The more clearly a destination's slogan reflects the uniqueness of its attractions, it has been demonstrated the more efficient a message it projects (Lee, Cai, & O'Leary 2005). Also, the slogans that create a concrete image, rather than the more generalized abstract images, deliver a cleaner and more effective brand image. While branding as the process of highlighting a unique identifier has been practiced less dynamically in destination marketing than in the general marketing arena (Cai 2002; Murphy, Benchendorff, & Moscardo 2007), its application and importance to destinations is becoming more widely recognized (Peirce & Ritchie 2007).

Disadvantages of the USP Approach

Despite all the beneficial effects of the USP indicated above, it is important to highlight a few caveats. The unstructured interviews conducted during the preliminary phase of this research gave indications of strains underlying the practice of the USP approach. Marketing literature has long identified the advantages of product diversity (Tallman& Li, 1996; Varadarajan 1986). By definition, a USP-based marketing approach may have the undesirable effect of narrowing the scope of attraction inventorying. Attractions that are part of a destination area not conforming to the USP definition might possibly be left out of the marketing campaigns. In centrally controlled tourism economies, the will of the prominent decision-making class will determine the extent of the USP adoption. In other situations, when the attraction clusters are competitive (low concentration of power for any single given attraction cluster), the political lobbying process among cluster stakeholders may well result in some USP based slogans not gaining prominence (Della Corte & Aria, 2016).

Attraction diversity (as opposed to attraction uniqueness) of a country has strategic, tactical, and operational benefits, and the USP based marketing campaigns could well be neglecting the value of such diversity. A diverse range of products can help a firm to spread the risk of market contraction and is particularly useful when a single star product offers no further opportunities for growth. Hence, while the USP based marketing approach is organic to small destinations with limited inherent attraction diversity, larger destination countries with a variety of attractions might find it less appealing. Attraction diversity and inter-attraction competitiveness within a destination country likely will determine the extent of USP adoption in its tourism campaigns.

Tourism Networks for Marketing Advantage

While small locally owned businesses are advocated, the problematic issue of whether small enterprises can survive in an increasingly competitive and globalized environment is answered in the affirmative by citing the idea of alliances (Gartner, 1999; Shaw, 2014). Experts have expressed serious doubts over the professed role of governments as altruistic and pro-people (van der Zee & Vanneste, 2015). On an average, nine out of 10 of the popular movements at the grassroots level were deemed illegal and suppressed by governments, observed Fox & Brown (1998).

Caribbean tourism is no different, as this research reveals Tourism SMEs have joined hands and formed networks to harness power against the powers that be. The effect of such networking is evident, at least to some extent, in governments and DMOs becoming more inclusive in their marketing campaigns.

Touristic products, especially eco-cultural ones, are more living systems than machines. Theme parks, may be more experienced through domination and control; however, the means of understanding more nature-based products, in which the essential characteristics include cooperative relationships, is through participation in the collective-sense-making process (Weidenfeld, 2013). A typical intermediary whose philosophy, mission, vision, and action are in dissonance with this might well adulterate the authentic experience sought after by the travelers (George & George, 2005; Strobl & Peters, 2013). Thus, disintermediation of such intermediaries, and substituting them with locally rooted cooperatives of small business owners could be useful in preserving the authentic spirit of touristic experience. If some of the Caribbean destinations have preserved the authentic in their USP statements or marketing campaigns in general, the influence of the collective bargaining power of the 'third way forces' has worked in its backdrop.

The Concept of Attraction Diversity

Product diversity is a key determinant of competitive advantage (Porter, 1990; Richard & Charles, 2013) and measuring the extent of monoculture of attractions is useful in analyzing destination competitiveness. Product diversity related studies are abundant in the economics and general marketing literature. Theoretical economists interested in competition related issues first investigated the topic of diversity (Hotelling 1929; Lerner & Singer 1937). Tallman and Li (1996) examined how product diversity impacts the performance of a firm and found a quadratic relationship. Wan and Hoskisson (2003) concluded that the home country environments moderate any such relationship. Fiegenbaum and Karnani (1991) observed the unique advantages of small-scale enterprises from diversifying their product offerings. These authors stressed that a diversified product portfolio is synonymous with output flexibility, a great asset in turbulent market conditions. Using economic theory, Rumelt (1982) predicted that the advantages of product diversity would still remain even after the effects of varying industry profitability were removed. However, the literature is not unified in its support for diversification. For example, Montgomery's (1985) advocacy for less diversified firms was built upon the premise that highly diversified firms have lower 'general market power' in their respective markets than do less diversified firms, even when they wield some 'specific market power.' Also, economists have often highlighted the inherent disharmony between efficiency and diversity (Chamberlin, 1933; Meade, 1974).

Leiper (1990) proposed the idea of a tourist attraction system and defined it as an emergent phenomenon resulting from the engagement between tourists and tourism related experiential resources. Attraction diversity is the extent of variance in attraction offerings and the basis for such variance (Lew, 1987). The extent of variance itself is multifaceted. In its simplest form, it can be seen linearly as variance within the same attraction type (or same core product). For example, a destination country may have different kinds of beaches that could be placed on a linear continuum from calm to rough beaches. This is represented in Figure 2.

B1	B2	B3	B4
C1	C2	C3	C4
Calmest beach			Roughest beach

Figure 2. Attraction Diversity as Linear Variance. Note. B 1-4 = beach types; C 1-4 =customer types

In this example, different customer types (C1, C2, C4, C4) are attracted to different beach types and the associated businesses (B1, B2, B3, B4) capitalize upon the differences in customer tastes. Another example, even more linear than the one given above, is that of two restaurants serving the same menu distinguishing their businesses based on differences in location and price.

Attraction diversity may also be modeled based on the 'convexity' of consumer preferences (Dixit & Stiglitz 1977). This takes into account that a consumer's preference for a compound product is not necessarily the sum total of consumer preference for each of the elements comprising the compound product. For example, a preference for coffee with cream and sugar may not be the sum of the individual preferences for coffee, cream, and sugar. It is not unusual to find a tourist fascinated by shopping and nature walks but not a nature walk dotted with shopping establishments. Similarly, tourists may prefer particular compound products even though they do not prefer some of the individual components of that mixture. Such emergence of synergy means that USP based promotions can work well even for destination countries having a diverse set of attractions. In these situations, USP slogans could be framed around the mixture, as long as the mixture is perceived as an emergent single attraction in the minds of tourists.

Even though diversity has remained on top of the literature over the past half-century, its definition was typically been assumed to be commonsense. According to Ranaivoson (2005), Sterling (1998) was one of the first to take serious initiates to operationalize the concept of 'diversity.' While Sterling (1998) did not define product diversity as such, his treatment of the term broadly included technological diversity and even biodiversity. He conceived diversity as being composed of three dimensions: variety, balance and parity. In the case of tourism destination countries, this could be visualized as given in Figure 3.

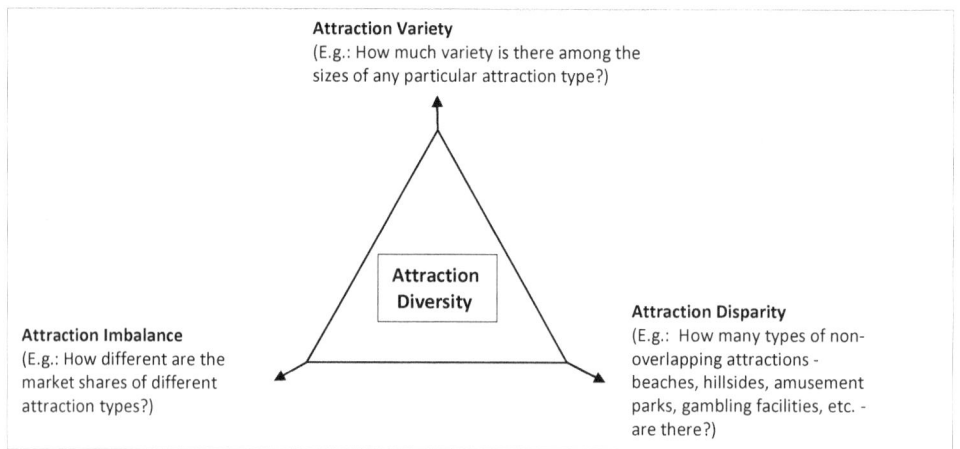

Figure 3. Attraction Diversity as a Multidimensional Construct

This Attraction Diversity scheme is presented essentially to demonstrate the complexity of how destinations could compete with others for tourist dollars. Oftentimes, it is assumed that attraction diversity is only a matter of its variety. Marketers, driven by this belief, tend to increase the variety of offerings while at the same time neglecting the associated dimensions of balance and parity. While variety is more tangle and measurable, the subtle impacts of the other two dimensions can negate any benefit that variety is likely to offer to a destination.

Summary

The business of tourism is truly multifaceted and an understanding of its nuances demands that we look beyond traditional disciplinary boundaries. As seen in the literature review, the context for this research is interdisciplinary that spans economics, sociology, psychology, politics, and environmental studies. This chapter attempted to position the research objectives in the context of the extant field of knowledge relevant for the present research. Gaps in the literature were identified. The hypotheses proposed in this research are potential solutions to address those gaps. The review of literature presented in this chapter has strengthened the plausibility of these hypotheses but also make a case for the need to subject them to further empirical examination.

Chapter 3: The Research Method

In this chapter, the methodology that guided the design of this study is discussed. Among the topics discussed are: the research design, research instrument development, population, sampling strategy, sample size, data collection procedures, and analytical methods.

Research Design

This research employed mixed methods. Qualitative and quantitative methods were used hand in hand and the results were integrated to address the research problem (Guest, 2013). Employing multi-methods was inevitable given the complexity of the issues under study. A single data source or data type could not have solved the issues under investigation. However, the quantitative and qualitative methods stood standalone: this researcher did not use mixed methods as a method for generalizing the exploratory findings in a two-stage research process (qualitative analysis followed by quantitative analysis).

Quantitative Phase

Data snapshots for USP slogans and tourism related national statistics for various Caribbean countries were taken in 2004, 2009, and 2014. Data were gathered towards the latter end of each of these years, generally considered as the beginning of the high season for Caribbean tourism. The Caribbean Tourism Organization's published secondary data was employed for this analysis. The data gathered covers all the Caribbean countries (the population of the study) and, given this, sampling was not attempted. In order to test the hypothesis involving moderation (H3), data for tourism arrivals in Jamaica was required. This data came from Jamaican Tourist Board / Visit Jamaica (JTB, 2015). Quantitative / Statistical analysis upon the secondary data was performed using SPSS / IBM - PASW Software. In particular, these analyses helped to test the hypotheses.

Qualitative Phase

Qualitative analysis upon the textual data was performed primarily using IBM's Watson Analytics software. However, computational software for qualitative analysis was used only as a decision support aid and not to replace the researcher's judgement. In terms of procedural steps, the marketing slogans of all members of the Caribbean Tourism Organization were examined, based both on the destinations' slogans on their own official tourism marketing websites, as well as the slogans used by the CTO promotional website. The slogans were shared with at least three marketing scholars who had expertise in the area of tourism marketing. These scholars were asked to classify each slogan into the most suitable level on the USP classification scheme proposed by Richardson and Cohen (1993). When there were disagreements among the experts, the median classification was used for further analysis. Additional data for qualitative analysis came in the form of tweets and TripAdvisor user reviews related to the Caribbean tourism, accessed using IBM Watson Analytics software's social media module. Qualitative data analysis for this project, therefore, included analyses of both text slogans and visual images (usually photographic) on the destinations' websites. Textual analysis followed, as closely as possible, Richardson and Cohen's (1993) liberal interpretation of uniqueness. Visual analysis focused primarily on the extent to which these destinations employed stereotypical and generic images of "sun & sand" tourism – sunny weather and sandy beaches being fairly ubiquitous commodities across the Caribbean region.

In addition, this researcher personally visited the Caribbean Tourism Organization annual conference in 2014 held during September 16-19 at Marriott Frenchman's Reef, US Virgin Islands, and interacted with the participants. The theme of the conference itself was *Realizing the Vision: Positioning Caribbean Tourism for Major Change*, a topic closely resonating with this study. Many of the participants were business owners, senior industry executives, government officials in tourism, or representatives of tourism nonprofits. In addition to numerous casual interactions, fourteen participants were interviewed extensively. Transcripts of the semi-structured interviews and informal interactions conducted with these stakeholders became the basis of much of qualitative analysis.

Procedure for the Development of the Attraction Diversity Index

Theoretical attempts to mathematically model product diversity are many. Although previous researchers have developed various product diversity measures (Grant, Jammine, & Thomas, 1988; Lewis & Winkler, 2015; Pitts & Hopkins, 1982), few if any are directly portable to measuring diversity of attractions in a tourism destination country. The studies mentioned above all refer to product diversity among tangible products and / or firms manufacturing these goods. However, while a country is not a company, nor is its attraction portfolio quite the same as the product portfolio of a company, the same basic framework used in traditional business contexts could still be adapted for tourism destination attraction diversity measurement.

Common approaches for measuring business diversity include the 'count approach' (Jacquemin & Berry 1979; Varadarajan & Ramanujam 1987) and the 'categorical approach' (Wrigley, 1970). The categorical approach subjectively classifies businesses into the categories of single business, dominant business, related business, and unrelated business (Rumelt, 1974). Two ratios were calculated: a specialization ratio (Rs = revenue attributable to the largest single business / total revenue), and a related ratio (Rr = revenue attributable to the largest group of related single businesses / total revenue). The values of these ratios were then used to determine the category of diversification. In practical terms, this approach presented difficulties. The relatedness between businesses are very subjective and even though overall revenues may be publicly available, data related to particular products, product lines, or related business groups are very hard to come by. Finally, for this current research, this approach was not well suited, since this approach focuses on the type of diversity rather than the degree of diversity.

Conversely, the count approach is focused on measuring the degree of product diversity. In its simplest form, diversity can be modeled as $D = N - 1$, where D is a measure of diversity and N represents the number of distinguishable products. Thus, in the special case of a destination country with only one attraction, $D = 0$.

The Herfindahl-Hirschman Index (HHI) provides a more robust operationalization of this approach (Hirschman, 1964; Matsumoto, Merlone, & Szidarovszky, 2012). This index measures the size of firms in relation to the industry and is an indicator of the amount of competition among them. That is,

$$H = \sum S_i^2$$

where S is the market share of firm 'i' in the industry. Typically, an H below 0.01 indicates a highly competitive, no concentration index.

An H below 0.15 indicates a largely un-concentrated index.

An H between 0.15 to 0.25 indicates moderate concentration.

An H above 0.25 indicates high concentration.

If all firms have an equal share of the market, the reciprocal of the index shows the number of firms in the industry. When firms have unequal shares, the reciprocal of the index indicates the "equivalent" number of firms in the industry. For the purpose of this study, HHI was used as a measure of the size of particular tourism attraction types in a country in relation to its overall tourism industry. An increase in HHI could be interpreted as a decrease in the product diversity (in this study, attraction type diversity) and vice versa (Kwoka Jr, 1985).

The tourism attraction diversity of a destination country is operationalized as the inverse of HHI. Mathematically, Attraction Diversity Index (ADI) is represented as:

$$ADI = 1/\sum (MS_i)^2$$

For example, MS_1 represents the market share of attraction cluster 1. Also, market share for a cluster = Revenue generated by the cluster / total tourism industry revenue for the country.

Construction of Attraction Cluster Equity (ACE)

Since HHI measures concentration, the inverse may be used to measure competition / diversity. Yet, tourism presents a distinctive case among industries. Using market shares of attraction types as the key determinants of diversity has certain notable downsides. For one thing, market share for particular attraction types reflects past marketing efforts and tourism policy priorities. Also, market share depends upon the singular aspect of revenue generation. Actually, misleading figures may result when some distinctly different attraction types do not figure highly on the revenue generation radar. Finally, in order to calculate ADI this way, it was necessary to

Table 1

An Example Demonstrating ACE Calculation

Attraction Type	Beach & Beach Activities	Cultural Heritage Attractions	Wilderness Attractions	Shopping, City, and Night Life	Business Attractions
Weighted Value of the Attraction Type	2 x 4.5 star beaches 3 x 3 star beach activities	1 x 4 star heritage attraction	1 x 3 star wildlife refuge	1 x 5 star night life	1 x 4 star business event location
Attraction Cluster Equity (ACE)	2x4.5+3x3=18 18/(18+4+3+5+4) = .52	1x4=4 4/(18+4+3+5+4) = .12	1x3=3 3/(18+4+3+5+4) = .09	1x5=5 5/(18+4+3+5+4) = .15	1x4=4 4/(18+4+3+5+4) = .12

overcome the operational difficulty of calculating revenues and market shares of individual attraction types. This led to the creation and operationalization of what would become the Attraction Cluster Equity (ACE) construct. The ACE is designed to measure the value of an attraction type for a destination country in a more meaningful way than the market share.

In order to calculate ACE, the top attractions in each country were determined as identified by TripAdvisor (www.tripadvisor.com) users. The top attractions for each country were classified into various known attraction categories. Then, each such classified attraction was weighted according to the aggregated 'stars' given for them (1 to 5 stars) by the users. In order to ensure that the aggregated star values were generalizable, no attraction with less than 30 stars was included. To explain this procedure better, the case of Jamaica is given below. The top nine attractions were classified into five clusters, as shown in Table 1. Each of these attractions in each cluster were weighed with their corresponding star values and then add these values to calculate the relative importance of that attraction cluster. Thus, mathematically:

Attraction Cluster Equity (ACE) =

Weighted value of the attraction type / $\sum$ Weighted values of all the attraction types.

Paradigmatic Assumptions

Social reality is complex and multifaceted (Yilmaz, 2013). An objective reality may be out there, or, may not be. What a person sees as reality is the only accessible reality for them. A person's knowledge is bounded in that the ontic reality is known to them only by means of their limited perceptions. Individuals are constrained to appreciate the truth from what they experience and thus, individuals are required to construct ontic truth from the epistemic roots (Golding & MacLeod, 2013).

The research presented here included elements of multiple paradigms. However, the 'pragmatic paradigm' (i.e., "truth is what is useful") guided the overall approach. This researcher held the view that multiple worldviews, even though mutually incompatible, can still co-exist to find solutions to the pricking problems affecting individuals and communities. Therefore, an eclectic approach to research involving real world business problems could draw from positivism, intrepretivism, constructivism, and from critical methods.

Quantitative analysis of secondary data and the statistical testing of various hypotheses included in this research were informed by the positivistic paradigm. The qualitative analysis based on open ended transcripts and social media feeds followed the interpretative paradigm. These analyses were tuned to appreciate how agents interpret cues and socially construct their realities. However, pragmatically, this researcher shifted perspectives between 'etic' and 'emic'. Doing so was expected to ensure balance in perspectives. Finally, when it came to understanding the complex dynamics of power relations among the destination stakeholder groups representing the tourism supply side, guidance given by the critical paradigm was deemed the most appropriate one.

Rights of the Participants and Legal Issues

A significant portion of the data used in this study was originally collected in connection with a larger research project on the Caribbean tourism. This researcher was the lead investigator of the research project. The University's review board was informed about the intention to use said data for this study, during the research prospectus development stage. In addition, the University was informed that none of the aforementioned secondary data included "private information" and, hence, did not involve human subjects.

Survey participants were presented with an informed consent form indicating approval by the University's Institutional Review Board. This form included a brief explanation of the purpose of the research, time commitments, risks involved, personal and societal benefits, researcher contact information, etc. The participants were explicitly told that their participation would be completely voluntary and that they could exit the survey any time.

Interviewees were asked for permission to be quoted before the interview took place. Data supplied by the subject matter experts were reported only when express permission was given, or the data was in the public domain (i.e., published). All subject matter experts were offered the opportunity to read the research thesis and/or the summary of their interview that are included in the thesis.

Summary

Informed by Laskey, Day, and Crask (1989) this researcher understood that a unique selling proposition is not merely what is said, but also how it is said. Overly reductionist research fails to recognize such differences in execution. Understanding that infusing quantitative analysis with qualitative insights is pivotal, this research utilized a mixed methods approach. Secondary data gathered from the Caribbean Tourism Organization and the Jamaican Tourist Board formed the basis of quantitative analysis. Primary interview data gathered from the Caribbean tourist industry stakeholders and qualitative data gathered from tourism review sites like TripAdvisor was used for qualitative analysis. The research was carried out in accordance with existing research protocols and best practice norms.

Chapter 4: Data Analysis and Findings

In Chapter 4, the results of the analysis of the data gathered for this study is presented. As indicated in the research methods chapter, this study followed mixed methods.

Tourism Promotional Slogans: A Word Cloud Analysis

A content analysis of the marketing slogans of various destination countries served as the initial stage of data analysis. Presented in Figures 4, 5, and 6 are the prominent words that appeared in the slogans of 2004, 2009 and 2014, respectively. Larger font sizes correspond to more frequently used words. Utilizing such a visual technique makes certain word patterns readily identifiable. However, in order to inventory the contextual polarity of text, a formal sentiment analysis was carried out. Analysis using IBM Many Eyes revealed that 57% of the words conveyed pleasant or positive moods, 18% of the words conveyed unpleasant or negative mood, while the remaining words were primarily neutral.

Figure 4. 2004 Slogan Word Cloud

The word 'Caribbean' appeared highly prominent across all slogans, across the study period. Most destinations countries recognize that they are the truest representatives of the spirit of the Caribbean. This way of defining uniqueness, however, loses some of its luster when all

Figure 5. 2009 Slogan Word Cloud

Figure 6. 2014 Slogan Word Cloud

destinations define as such. If Country A's USP slogan included word phases containing the word "Caribbean," as if the true spirit of the Caribbean is unique to Country A; however, similar word phasing was also contained in the USP slogans of County B and Country C, the effect is the nullification of the potential relative benefits for all.

A review of the word clouds reveals some interesting overall trends. Caribbean destinations are increasingly portraying themselves as much more than just sun, beaches and beachside resorts. In particular, the word 'nature' has become more popular in the slogans of various countries. As is visible in Figure 7, the heaviest use of USP oriented advertising peaked in 2009. Year 2014 data showed a few countries dropping out of the USP based campaigns (USP level=0), some lowering the levels of USP employed, while a few newcomers, like Cuba, joining the USP bandwagon.

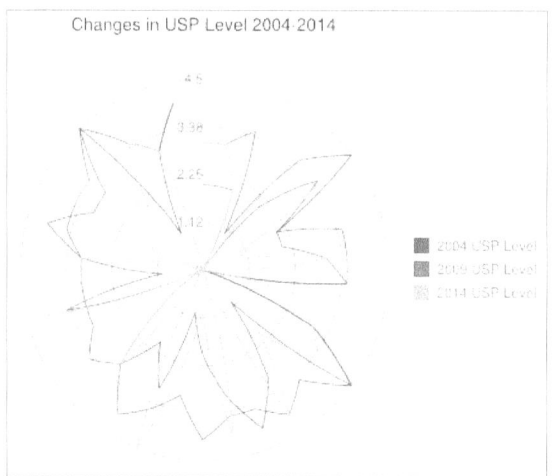

Figure 7. Changes in the levels of USP used over 2004-2014.

As Table 2 implies, despite its relative prominence, the use of the word 'Caribbean' dropped substantially. By 2014, countries were looking to become more unique and singular, not so ubiquitous as in previous years. Another interesting observation is that slogans in 2014 have become more representative of more tangible aspects of the destination experience: words like secret, paradise, and treasure have largely been eliminated.

Analysis of Social Media Content about the Caribbean Tourism

To corroborate these findings, IBM's *Watson Analytics©* was used to generate a heat map of social media activities related to the Caribbean tourism. In particular, recent tweets about the Caribbean tourism was analyzed. Only tweets for three years (2013-2015) were available for analysis. Of the 2,875 tweets, 1,219 conveyed positive mood, 764 were neutral, while the remaining 892 contained negative sentiments. Tweets related to certain country destinations had more positivity than others (Jamaica, Turks & Caicos, Barbados, Aruba, St. Lucia, Cayman, St. Martin, US Virgin Islands, in descending order).

Table 2

Most common words across tourism slogans

Keyword	Frequency/Year		
	2004	2009	2014
Caribbean	12	6	5
Island	6	3	4
Experience	2		
Secret	2		
Little	2		
Explore	2		
Paradise	2	5	3
French	2	2	
Nature	2	2	2
Treasure	2		
Beautiful	2		

Note: These numbers represent the number of slogans in which each of these keywords occur.

Based on topics, a substantial number of tweets were directly or indirectly related safety and security. Thorny issues in guest-host relations were particularly evident. This was followed by references to nature (especially, topics like the cleanliness of beaches, noise levels, wildlife, and water pollution). Interestingly, less than 20 of all the tweets analyzed had any mention of culture or indigenous lifestyle; seven of them (likely by repeat visitors) lamented about the degradation of the Caribbean destinations over the years. Interestingly, almost none of the tweets made during 2013-2015 directly mentioned the official marketing slogans. This posed the question of whether the new generation *Tourists 2.0* actually care about official marketing efforts (Camprubí, Guia, & Comas, 2013). Evidences from various studies show that contemporary tourists are more likely to be guided by peer traveler reviews (word of mouth) and their own research than official or even 'expert' opinions.

The top 10 countries in the Caribbean as per the 2014 best tourism destination reviews by TripAdvisor users are given in Table 3.

Table 3

TripAdvisor User Reviews of the Caribbean Destinations, 2014

Destination	Review Excerpts	Top 1 Attraction	Top 2 Attraction	Top 3 Attraction
Jamaica	Is there anything better than stretching out like a cat in a warm patch of...	Seven Mile Beach	Negril Cliffs	Mayfield Falls
Providenciales, Turks and Caicos	The most populated of the Turks and Caicos islands, Providenciales is one of the...	Grace Bay	Taylor Bay Beach	Chalk Sound
Puerto Rico	Puerto Rico offers the perfect balance of rum-soaked nightlife and tranquil...	Flamenco Beach	San Juan National Historic Site	Old San Juan
Barbados	Romance and adventure are in the air on this lush West Indian island in the...	Hunte's Gardens	Carlisle Bay	St. Nicholas Abbey
Aruba	Aruba is the quintessential Caribbean island, all sun and sea and stretches of...	Eagle Beach	Philip's Animal Garden	Arikok National Park

St. Lucia	When was the last time you went out for a casual drive and ended up inside a...	Treetop Adventure Park	Tet Paul Nature Trail	Pitons
Grand Cayman	The farther you go from Grand Cayman's busy docks, the more peace and quiet...	Stingray City	Seven Mile Beach	Cayman Spirits Co. Distillery
St. Maarten-St. Martin	Get the experience of visiting two island colonies in the same 37 square miles....	Maho Beach	Orient Bay Beach	Yoda Guy Movie Exhibit
St. John, U.S. Virgin Islands	Ecotourism is alive and kicking on St. John. There's more than enough to do on...	Maho Beach	Trunk Bay	Cinnamon Bay
Antigua, Antigua and Barbuda	Antigua has hundreds of beaches, from the bustling Pigeon Point to the...	Stingray City	Valley Church Beach	Nelson's Dockyard

The word cloud analysis of the top reviews is presented in Figure 8.

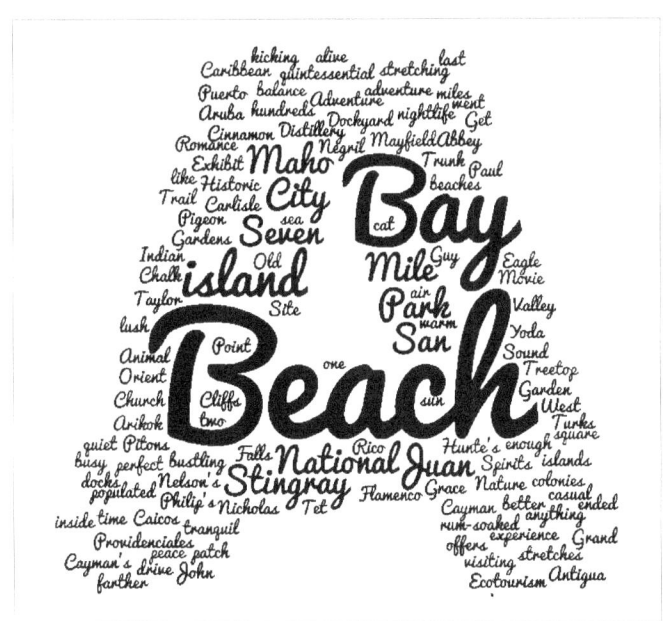

Figure 8. Word Cloud of Trip Advisor User Reviews, 2014

These reviews are interesting because of the continued prominence of terms like beach

and bay, even in 2014, despite the fact that the official line for tourism promotion has moved to apparently more enlightened products such as nature and culture. Perhaps the visitors to the Caribbean still consider these destinations predominantly as beach destinations and nothing more. If so, marketers need to conclude that the official remarketing campaigns have not succeeded in achieving their stated objectives.

Despite the above, some diversity in the perceptions of tourists cannot be overlooked. For example, the number one attraction for Barbados was Hunte's Gardens; for St. Lucia, it was Treetop Adventure Park; for Cayman, Antigua, and Bermuda, it was Stingray City. Non-beach attractions as well are figured in the top two and top three lists. Notwithstanding, in the descriptive comments, beaches and beach life considered top attractions over everything else.

Differences in the Use of USP Levels across Time Periods

In order to quantify the significance of the changes in the use of USP levels across the decade, one-way ANOVA were performed upon the USP level data. The hypothesis tested was that no significant changes occurred in the levels of USP used across 2004, 2009 and 2014 (formally stated in Chapter 1, hypothesis section). As seen in Table 4, the null hypothesis was rejected ($p < 0.05$). Thus, the implication is that significant changes in the level of USP used occurred across the time frame of the study period.

Table 4

Statistical Significance of the Changes in the USP Levels

ANOVA

Source of Variation	df	SS	MS	F	Significance F
Regression	2	15.55	7.775	4.899	0.0189
Residual	99	157.1	1.587		
Total	101	172.7			

Table 5

Range of USP Values in 2004, 2009, and 2014

USP Level	2004	2009	2014
Highest	4.50	4.50	4.50
Lowest	0.00	0.00	0.00
Mean	2.50	3.21	2.29
Standard Deviation	1.28	0.91	1.51

These results confirm the earlier finding that the year 2009 saw the peak of the USP based marketing campaigns (both highest mean USP and lowest standard deviation). Likewise, during the 2009-2014 period, a decrease in the USP level and an associated increase in divergence in the levels across nations can be observed. The analysis, thus, prompts us to make a revision of the hypothesis (H1) that there is a continued increase in the use of USPs over the years. Hypothesis 1 is partially true (the increase continued until 2009) but then the trend reversed, as evidenced by the 2014 data.

How Attraction Diversity is Related to the Extent of USP Use

To examine the relationship between attraction diversity and USP use, straight lines (y=mx+c) were fitted over the data available. Since what the data included the entire population, a statistical testing of significance of this relationship was deemed unnecessary. Three equations were derived based on the data for 2004, 2009 and 2014 (x=attraction diversity index; y=USP level):

2004

$y = 0.117128x + 1.972817$

2009

$y = 0.161789x + 2.477685$

2014

$y = -0.126659x + 2.864197$

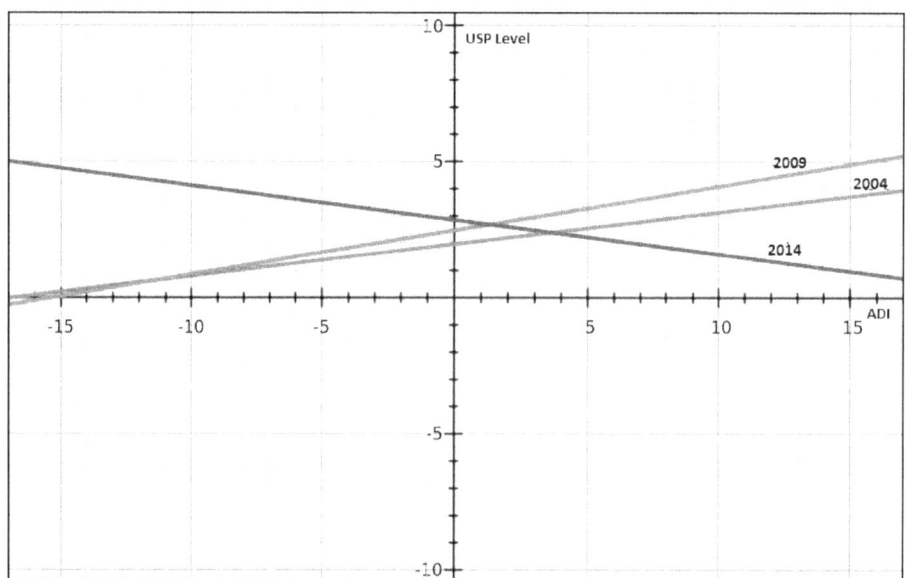

Figure 9. USP Level as a Function of Attraction Diversity

Interestingly, the expected relation was true only for the 2014 data (see Figure 9). Possibly, this implies that tourism marketing over the years has become more of a negotiated and democratic process. Smaller attraction types might not have wielded the same lobbying power over the marketing policy authorities in the past. An alternative explanation is that tourism authorities understand the harms of highly targeted and narrowly specified USP based campaigns for their destinations.

While the 2014 data shows attraction concentration measured in terms of ACE indicates an overall trend, the trend is the resultant of multidirectional currents at the country levels: some countries with really low attraction concentration have low USPs. In addition, a few countries with above average diversity still go for relatively higher levels of USP implementation than their peers (see Figure 10).

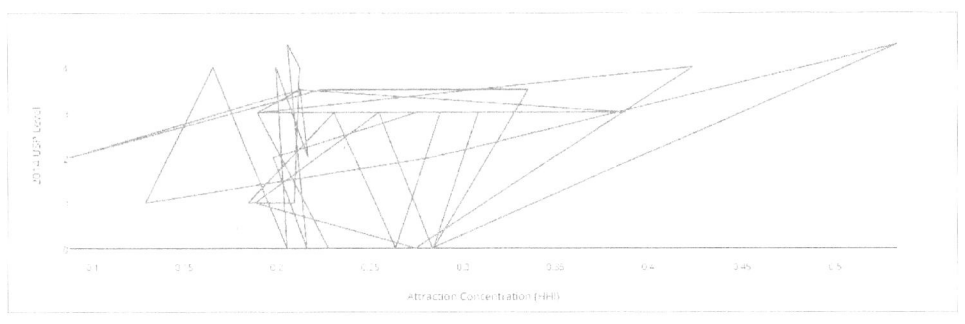

Figure 10. Attraction Concentration – 2014 USP level distribution

The second hypothesis (H2), thus, stands supported only for the 2014 data. During 2004 and 2009, the correlation between attraction diversity and USP level used was positive. It could be the awareness that highlighting USPs do not work in attraction diverse destinations that made destination marketers to rethink about this. However, more research is needed to make this assertion.

Attraction Diversity, USP, and Tourist Choice

One element examined was if attraction diversity predicts arrival figures. The result was negative overall (R^2=0.00164, Sig=0. 0.820123). Given that the data explored included the entire population, lack of statistical significance did not need to be considered as an issue. This analysis shows higher diversity does not mean higher arrivals, which makes sense since most tourists come to a Caribbean destination with a single type of attraction in mind and the marketing direction for each island nation is probably to offer the best in terms of that single unique attraction that it has.

Based on the theoretical premise that the adoption of USP is an effective marketing strategy and that attraction diversity dilutes the effectiveness of the USP approach, the composite model was tested. In this model, ADI is positioned as the mediating variable, USP as the predictor variable, and tourist arrivals as the dependent variable. According to Baron and Kenny (1986), "A moderator is a qualitative or quantitative variable that affects the direction and/or strength of the relation between an independent or predictor variable and a dependent or criterion variable" (p.27). In other words, a moderating variable (Z) explains *when* X is related to Y.

In simple cases of multiple regressions, the two predictors are in an additive relationship with the criterion (Pedhazur, 1982). That is, the relationship between X and Y is not fundamentally changed by including Z in the prediction equation. Nor is the impact of Z altered by the inclusion of X. The two effects, therefore, can be simply added together. When variables exert only straightforward additive effects, they are referred to as main effects. However, sometimes the effect of one predictor is changed based upon the addition of a second predictor. Perhaps the relationship between X and Y is strong and positive when Z is absent, but weak when Z is present. Or, perhaps the relationship between X and Y is positive when Z is present and negative when Z is absent. In these examples, the relationship between X and Y is conditioned or moderated by Z. In essence, Z regulates the relationship between X and Y. X and Z are known to interact, since the effect of each variable is dependent on the effect of the other (McClelland & Judd, 1993). X and Z work together to predict Y. The importance of Z is not that it directly impacts the dependent variable, it may or it may not. Rather Z matters because it influences the relationship between X and Y. Either X or Z could be termed the moderator, depending on theory.

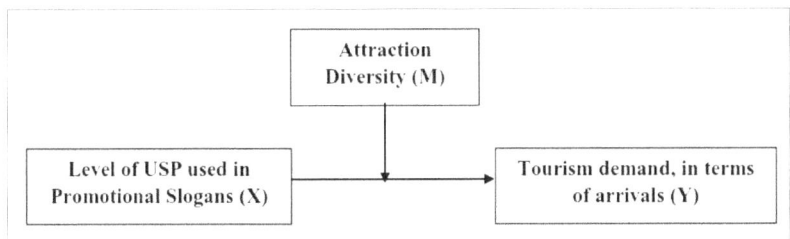

Figure 11. USP-Tourist Demand, Moderated by Attraction Diversity

Analysis of combined data for all time segments under study revealed that the interaction term (ADI) alone explained 13.6% of the variance at a significance level of $p<0.05$, which is sufficient to establish moderation. However, given the divergence in the literature on moderation, two further regressions were performed: USP level alone, which explained 22.7% of variance in the arrival figures ($p<0.05$); and, USP x ADI, which together explained 34.1% of the variance ($p<0.05$). The interaction product introduces a considerable level of improvement in the variance explained. The models are summarized in Table 6. Thus, the third hypothesis is supported. Attraction diversity has a moderating influence upon the effectiveness of the USP approach, as evidenced by the way it attenuates the relationship between the level of USP employed and the tourist arrivals

Table 6

Testing of Moderation by ADI

Model	R	R Square	Adjusted R^2	Standard Error of Estimate
1*	.369	.136	.135	.92138
2**	.476	.227	.225	.78127
3***	.589	.347	.346	.71934

Note *= ADI predicting arrivals; ** = USP predicting arrivals; *** = ADI x USP predicting arrivals

Hidden Undercurrents in the Determination of the USP

In order to address the fourth research question (RQ4: How do businesses differentiate themselves within the homogeneity implied by their destination's USP statement?), qualitative interview data was gathered. Content analysis of open ended qualitative interviews that the researcher held with the participants of the CTO Annual Conference (2014) held during September 16-19, 2014, indicated the complexity of the process leading to a USP determination in many countries. While anonymity requirements and various situational constraints prohibit the researcher from naming particular interviewees, the outcome of this process was enlightening. A few interesting themes have emerged from these interviews:

Theme 1: The Power of Networks

A top official of the Jamaican tourism board stated this:

P1: The tourism industry association here is very powerful. And, within the association, there are informal lobbying groups representing different product categories. Say, the promoters of high end spas or scuba diving businesses could be groups with their unique interests. The political class has got nefarious connections with some of these groups.

These groups directly pressurize public policy makers to sway things in their favor. They do this also through their voice in the industry association. ().

Small businesses have their associations representing their interests. Two small business promoters from Bahamas, with whom together the researcher had a conversation, agreed:

P2 & P3: Our strength is not our money. We don't have much of it. Our strength is our number. We are massive. We are the vote bank for our politicians. They can't abandon us. Our interest is that our small and unique tourism businesses should not be slaughtered by the massive all-inclusives. Politicians will be on their path of career suicide by alienating us.

Theme 2: Media Relations

Local media is tapped into this fray as well. Some businesses give the media more advertisements. Many media houses survive primarily from this revenue. Then, there is unconfirmed reports of media being paid to promote for and against particular forms of tourism development. The marketing director of one of the Dominican Republic based all-inclusive resorts confided the following:

P4: We know that advertising in the local media is not going to bring us international visitors. Local visitors already know us and there is no much benefit in advertising, either. In any case, we don't get local customers. Yet, we advertise heavily in the local media - just because we are not allowed to openly bribe them. Media according to us is the primary agent for building public opinion. We want them to represent our interests. Advertising is a bridge. In addition to helping us build good community reputation, they also give our people airtime in news discussions. You will know the value of it only when you read about some otherwise successful businesses that had to be closed due to the public wrath.

Another way of looking at this is that advertising locally is a way of a community to support the very community that they serve and which serves them; contributing to the news media is supporting the central public education/watchdog of the community. Newspapers can be considered a community builder - so it's good business to support your local paper.

Nonetheless, these practices raise the issue of ethics. When the media supports the unique interest propositions of particular businesses and business clusters for reasons other than fairness of justice, and when people or governments are influenced by such unbalanced public support, that is a disastrous path. While it is hard to conclude such practices exist rampantly based merely on a few interviews, to add credence to these allegations the researcher inquired about this supposed situation with a few small scale business owners (P3, P4, P5), who also implied this happens as a norm in the Caribbeans and that "everyone knows about it".

Theme 3: Politics of Populism and Nepotism

State governance also is an important factor in the cultural politics of tourism (Light, 2007). Effectively, governments decide the national USP choice. A government's promotion of tourism not only can heighten the cultural self-consciousness and ethnic pride of indigenous groups, but also can suppress those groups that are not selected, according to Wood (1984). Tourism promotion is a twin edged sword that needs to be handled carefully. Governments are known to support their voter base or the elites, according to the power dynamics in a particular situation.

A State Tourism Information Officer commented,

P6: Officers have virtually no role in the determination of USPs. It is the political class that makes these decisions. I have data that says one thing, but it is never asked. Politicians in power often represent various regions and businesses and decisions are influenced by these considerations.

The competitive struggles for a voice work in a myriad of ways. Whether these struggles are good for the overall health of the industry is an entirely different issue. Politics often is seen as a legitimized means of protecting the elite interests. Although politics and tourism are strongly interrelated, the former shaped the latter more often and did not always contribute to the development of the industry, as noted by Altinay and Bowen (2006). The selectivity involved in destination promotion might further perpetuate power disparities among social groups and, in particular, limit ethnic minority actor roles (Palmer, 2007). This selectivity implied through the choice of USPs could trigger negatively deviant behavior among the industry players.

Tourism promotion is the result of a power play; identification of images representing destinations is a politically charged and negotiated process and the sub-texts of promotional messages have imprints of the political struggles (Henderson, 2003). The importance and function of the tourism image must be understood in its wider socio-political and cultural role, observed Morgan and Pritchard (1998). The creation and representation of place is a social process. By its very, nature tourism is explicitly related to notions of place through tourism promotion and development (Hall, 2003).

Theme 4: Survival of the Fittest

A topic of special interest for the researcher during the conversations was the way small businesses which do not align well with the national tourism campaign's central message, embodied in USPs and other communication strategies, deal with the situation. Many participants reacted to this and two noteworthy responses are paraphrased below:

P7:Tourists make up their minds on what to see, what to expect, etc. And, for the Caribbean, this is all well-set. Sun, Sea, Sand, Sex. It's so bland, but deeply ingrained in the tourist imaginations. I risk losing business if I don't fit my business with this theme.

A small resort owner based in Angola narrated how she had to close down a farm tourism operation she conceived and developed:

P8: My uncle had a big greenhouse based farm that hosted a wide variety of local vegetables and I encouraged him to remodel it so that tourists staying at my resort could visit them. He also grew ostrich and chicken in the farm. He took a loan and did exactly what I said. I prepared a pamphlet and kept at the reception of the resort; also incentivized my front desk person to promote the farm visit. Sadly, not even a single tourist showed any interest. Finally, I personally met a family from India that was eating in my restaurant who told me the food was delicious. I asked them if they would want to see from where the food came. With some reluctance, thus I made it possible for the first tourist visit to the farm. But, it is so hard to sustain this kind of business here.

Tourism opportunities have actually dented agriculture in countries like Aruba, by raising the prices of agricultural labor. This respondent's uncle, however, made some money by selling the local grown vegetables to her resort. That said, many farmers are faced with the choice of whether to continue farming or to sell land to the resort developers.

Summary

The analysis presented in this chapter highlights a range of issues associated with the USP experiment that the Caribbean countries ushered in tourism. The researcher took snapshot data for 2004, 2009, and 2014 to compare and contrast the approach to the use of USPs. Was the experiment a success or failure? Given that actual tourism demand is the result of myriad forces and controlling all of them for a USP's singular contribution is impractical. There are clear winners and losers in the USP oriented campaign eras that this research investigated.

Hence, a more robust way to think about marketing approaches like the adoption of USP is that these reflect the subjective understandings and priorities of tourism decision makers from time to time. Priorities in particular are the results of a negotiated political process and this is evident from the way policy makers are seeing the whole situation. That said, there has been a general move away from USP oriented branding of tourism destination in the Caribbean. Of course, this shift is more evident in attraction diverse destinations. Again, while the shift is happening, alternatives are not evident. Various community oriented small scale tourism projects have come up with their innovative marketing approaches: but, it is unlikely such models will replace the dominant 4S (Sun, Sea, Sand, Sex) model of beachside-centric mass tourism. Tourism destinations in the Caribbean region need to find out newer bases of competitive advantage and the search for such bases is likely to continue

Chapter 5: Conclusion

Caribbean tourist destinations increasingly are realizing the need to collaborate together for the tourist. The Caribbean Tourism Organization has been encouraging member nations to identify elements that make each of them unique so that marketing dollars are not wasted in competing against one another (Hill & Lewis, 2015). Still, for the mass tourist, the Caribbean is still a single, largely indistinguishable, region. The geography and climate in the Caribbean region varies, however, not so much distinguishable to the gaze of the touristic eyes. National destination management organizations and tourism industry bodies of each country in the Caribbean have struggled to differentiate their country from all others, but again with little success.

Overall Results

Based on data gathered in 2004, 2009, and 2014, the researcher observed how different Caribbean destinations have experimented with the use of USPs. The high octane use of USP based advertisement peaked around 2009 and then declined, based on the 2014 data. The honeymoon with USP oriented advertising peaked in 2009. Given the need to differentiate offerings and to stand out, it is intuitive to understand the logic behind the USP based campaigns. However, the question is whether these campaigns really benefitted. Even when the highest level of use of USPs was noted for a country, the benefits could not have been great because many other countries had almost similar content in their USP messages.

The Caribbean destinations increasingly are realizing that they are not just beaches and beachside resorts. In particular, the word 'nature' has become more popular in the slogans of various countries. Year 2014 data also shows many countries dropped out of the unique selling proposition based campaigns, many moderating their extreme views on uniqueness, while a few

newcomers like Cuba joined the USP bandwagon (their modest slogan was 'Autentica Cuba').
The findings do not mean that Caribbean destinations are losing steam on differentiation; what
was observed from this research is that the basis of differentiation is not as enthusiastically
communicated via the USP slogans today, as it was half a decade back.

Revisiting the Research Questions

The research questions proposed to be addressed in this study are restated below, along
with summarized solutions.

RQ1: *As the Caribbean country destinations continue to evolve and mature, whether
there is still a continuing trend toward the increasing use of the USP approach?*

The USP use, operationalized in terms of the grade of marketing slogans / DMO taglines,
increased during preparation of the early paper of the study period. USP use peaked by 2009 but
hence started its decline. Most Caribbean destinations appeared now to be heading towards an
era of mass-customized selling propositions. Advances in information and communication
technologies have aided tourism marketers tremendously in this regard – to the extent that, now
it is possible to customize marketing slogans at an individual traveler level. Actually, tourism
related websites and apps capture user behavior and tailor-make their entire offerings each
individual customer in a fully automated manner.

RQ2: *What is the relation between the attraction diversity of a destination management
area and the level of USP usage in that destination area's promotional campaigns?*

Generally speaking, an inverse relationship was observed, increasingly true towards the
latter part of the study period. This trend is understandable, given that diverse destinations may
find it difficult to pick up any single selling proposition. However, there are exceptions. Some
island destinations have included in their "unique" selling propositions many items, and these

USP statements generally adhere to the general proposition that "diversity is our uniqueness". Theoretically, however, such framing may not stand up to the rigorous definition of what might constitute a USP statement.

RQ3: *In the context of cruise tourism in the Caribbean, does the choice of USP used in the destination marketing campaign or a destination's attraction diversity impact tourist choice?*

Yes, both affect tourist choice. Analysis in terms of overall tourist arrivals across the decade from 1994-2004 indicate that USP use is positively related to tourist arrivals. Attraction diversity, however, intervened as a moderating variable dampened the direct impact of USP upon arrivals. USP use may have another interesting consequence, as emerged from some of the qualitative interviews. In attraction diverse destination countries, the use of USP based marketing is related to a larger gap between tourist expectations and performance. In other words, USPs seem to 'mislead' tourists. Recalling that the difference between Performance – Expectation is customer satisfaction (Parasuraman, Zeithaml, & Berry, 1994), this finding may have an important implication for destination marketers and marketing scholars alike.

RQ4: *How do businesses differentiate themselves within the homogeneity implied by their destination's USP statement?*

In most destinations, there are businesses that are clearly beneficiaries of the USP based campaigns. These are generally businesses whose products and services align with the USP slogans. However, the qualitative interviews reveal that other businesses feel the heat, and they feel isolated and discriminated in this approach. Actually, businesses aligned with different attraction types (e.g., beach shacks; downtown entertainment; nightlife) form their lobby groups to sway the national level tourist marketing campaigns. Interview participants confided that many big properties are maintained by people connected with powerful politicians or top bureaucrats and hence, national campaigns often sway to their benefit. Yet, smaller property owners have often formed cooperative marketing arrangements to counteract this.

Implications for Theory

Studies on the use of USP's in tourism are not many, a search would reveal (Blain, Levy, & Ritchie, 2005; Deslandes & Goldsmith, 2015; Shanka, 2001). This research made a unique contribution in understanding how USP slogans are influenced by the diversity of attractions in a destination area. What helped in furthering this understanding was the development of attraction diversity and attraction cluster indices (ADI & ACE) by the present researcher. These two complementary concepts are conspicuous by their absence in the destination management literature (George, Henthorne, and Williams, 2016; Henthorne, George, and Miller, 2016). This research is the first lead in identifying and filling that vacuum. As a first step, it was demonstrated how ADI-ACE could be used to quantify the extent of monoculture of attractions and how marketing strategies get determined by its concentrating power. This preliminary effort should provide avenues for future researchers to refine these indices and employ them in the analysis of various issues related to competition and diversity in tourism destination areas.

The extant theory was incrementally improved with the identification of certain thus-far-unknown relations, such as the moderating role of attraction diversity in the effectiveness of USP use. This research shows that the diversity of attraction types in a destination area make the application of USP based promotions problematic. In addition, this research gives preliminary indications that tourist satisfaction could be adversely affected if a highly attraction diverse destination promotes itself with a single USP and if tourists who buy into the same get disconfirmations when they actually make their visits.

Another contribution this research provides to theory is in clarifying an understanding about tourism network formation. Evidence gathered for this study indicates the dynamics of developing cooperative societies among tourism SMEs in the Caribbean. A fundamental drive for cooperatives is that they fetch the small and medium businesses leverage in dealing with large scale enterprises that are often backed by powerful players in the industry (Cai, 2002). These networks also have given some marketing advantage for the SMEs, like the use of a shared web portal for destination marketing (Shaw, 2014; Strobl, & Peters, 2013).

Implications for Practice

The special benefits of a USP based national tourism campaign for businesses that are aligned with the agreed upon definition of the USP needs further exploration. Such businesses can potentially leverage the benefits of the government funded campaign with relatively low promotional budgets. This has significant implications for further tourism development in a country, too. Similarly, the disadvantages of the USP approach for destinations with attraction diversity are evident. From a managerial practice point of view, unless the inherent contradictions among the stakeholders in a diverse destination cannot be resolved with a higher order understanding / harmonization, promoting any singular USP is counterproductive.

Destination marketers should be aware that attraction diversity can reduce the benefits of USP based campaigns, and at worse can mislead potential tourists about what a destination could offer. In some cases, however, attraction diversity could pleasantly surprise people, leading to delight. However, it is more likely that tourists attracted to a destination because of its uniqueness are unimpressed by the accidental diversity. This could lead to dissatisfaction, complaining behavior, and behavioral disloyalty (Weiermair & Peters, 2000). Generally, it is preferable that tourists are pleasantly surprised, observes Galani-Moutafi (2000). Marketing that promises one thing and delivers something else will not be sustainable; in the context of this research, for destination managers, this means not to highlight uniqueness when it does not exist.

Again, from the practitioner perspective, it is timely to examine the possibilities of mass-customized USP campaigns, identifying each individual tourist, understanding his or her expectations in terms of destination experience, and co-creating the offerings available at the destination that resonate with their expected experience (Binkhorst & Den Dekker, 2009). As the social media conversation analysis included in this research indicates, there is a notable gap between what destination marketers consider as USPs and what tourists consider are the key values of destinations (Rihova, Buhalis, Moital, & Gouthro, 2015). Huang, Backman, Backman, & Chang (2016) notes that recent advances in information and communication technologies (ICTs) permit custom making marketing messages in line with the tourist aspirations. An encouraging sign is that, keeping this objective in mind, the Caribbean Tourism Organization (CTO) began performing big data analysis on mined tourist data from diverse sources, including the social media.

Directions for Further Research

Businesses that traditionally marketed attractions which were not in conformity with the official USP statement could possibly realign their products and services. If not, the alternative question is how such businesses would differentiate themselves within the homogeneity implied by the USP statement. Evidences that come from some of the peripheral regions in the Caribbean indicate that the peripheral regions are moving out of the fast paced beach tourism model to various 'slow tourism' alternatives that include promoting sustainable living experiences, eco-farming, and cultural tourism (Timms & Conway, 2012). A recommendation is that these outlier businesses and regions could benefit by forming cooperative community networks of their own and market their regions based on the synergy implied by such cooperation.

Advances in information and communication technologies may have led to firms finding ways to reach different customer segments with different USPs (Ashley & Tuten, 2015). Some even anticipate the extreme of this situation, which would be a mass customized marketing communication system capable of delivering individualized selling propositions. The trend of what this researcher would call 'Individualized Selling Propositions (ISPs) is already visible; marketers are on a move from propositions unique to products to those unique to the individual customers. Questions remaining are concerned with what this technological trend means for destination marketing in the Caribbean and beyond, and if countries are catching up with this revolution. The researcher's pilot observations in the field were somewhat puzzling. The private tourism businesses have already caught up with the ISP model mentioned above while the government controlled national tourism bodies, tasked with marketing an entire country, still live by the traditional USP era. More research is required to better understand the situation and possibly to find ways for realigning marketing at these two levels.

Ironically, one of the surprising findings of this study is not in its pre-hypothesized findings. During the literature review phase of this study, a lot of research related to cruising in the Caribbean was identified and it was expected that cruising would pop up prominently in the qualitative analysis as an important topic. However, neither in the USP slogans nor in the popular tweets or destination reviews, did the term cruise or cruising find a key mention. This observation was serendipitous, given that cruise tourism is still the lifeblood of the Caribbean tourism (Henthorne, George, & Smith, 2013). Perhaps the reason for cruise or cruising not being mentioned may be the terms are considered 'default', and that there is nothing extraordinary to talk about with regard to either. More research is needed to better understand this trend.

Limitations of the Study

One key limitation of this study was the dependence of secondary and tertiary data for a significant chunk of analysis. Even though primary qualitative data was used to triangulate the analysis, the extent of data collection was not sufficient to fully justify the requirement for "theoretical saturation" (O'Reilly & Parker, 2012). Also, the researcher used data gathered at three snapshot points (2004, 2009, 2014) to derive generalized conclusions about events on a continuous scale. An associated limitation is the use of such non-experimental data to test hypotheses that propose causal relations.

The process of classifying USPs at various levels in a hierarchy involved a lot of subjective judgement. Colleagues of the researcher who had competence in tourism marketing theory assisted with this process, which helped to ensure essential face validity. However, these colleagues did not possess significant expertise in the nuances of the Caribbean tourism and, therefore, their judgements were plausibly challengeable. Difficulties in translating slogans from Spanish to English before arranging them in the hierarchy might have added an extra layer of error. Also, it was not possible for the researcher to identify and isolate various intervening variables confounding the relations tested. Given these limitations, the findings of this study should be extrapolated with caution.

Finally, while strictly not a limitation of this study, the researcher was aware of the fact that a holistic examination of concepts and their relationships in the specified area of inquiry was not carried out in this research. While the research interlinked attraction diversity and unique selling proposition, these constructs potentially also are linked with various other constructs in the knowledge field. Examination of some of these linkages would have thrown further light upon the actual research problem itself.

Concluding Remarks

The underpinnings of tourism phenomenon are often found in place-related constructs such as distance and diversity (George & George, 2004). Tourism researchers must understand, in operational terms, how these place-related variables influence tourist behavior. In this regard, one important issue is how travelers and tourism businesses perceive the concept of diversity and uniqueness of attractions pinned to places called tourism destinations and respond to their perceptions (George, Inbakaran, & Poyyamoli, 2010).

This research explored a few key issues hitherto unknown in the corresponding literature. In particular, the construct of attraction diversity was proposed and an index to quantify it was developed. Also, a number of hypotheses related to unique selling propositions and attraction diversity were tested. In addition, the qualitative / explorative part of the inquiry helped the researcher propose a few hitherto unknown relations in the extant literature. Future researchers can carry this lead by probing further into the various other issues surrounding unique selling propositions and attraction diversity.

References

Aaker, D. (1991). *Managing brand equity: Capitalizing on the value of a brand name*. New York, NY: Free Press.

Aaker, D., & Joachimsthaler, E. (2000). *Brand leadership: The next level of the brand revolution*. New York, NY: Free Press.

American Marketing Association. (2014). Dictionary: Unique selling proposition (USP). Retrieved from http://www. marketingpower. com/_layouts/dictionary. aspx of 31 December 2015.

Anfuso, G., Williams, A. T., Hernández, J. C., & Pranzini, E. (2014). Coastal scenic assessment and tourism management in western Cuba. *Tourism Management, 42*, 307-320.

Apergis, N., & Payne, J. E. (2012). Research note: Tourism and growth in the Caribbean– evidence from a panel error correction model. *Tourism Economics, 18*(2), 449-456.

Arseculeratne, D., & Yazdanifard, R. (2014). How green marketing can create a sustainable competitive advantage for a business. *International Business Research, 7*(1), 130-142.

Baker, D. M. A., & Stockton, S. (2013). Caribbean cruise tourism: Issues, challenges and sustainability. *Studies of Organisational Management & Sustainability, 1*(2), 79-97.

Baker, J. (2016). Black like me: Caribbean tourism and the St. Kittsmusic festival. *Ethnomusicology, 60*(2), 263-278.

Bao, Y., & Shao, A. T. (2002). Nonconformity advertising to teens. *Journal of Advertising Research, 42*(3), 56-65.

Barker, D. (1998). Geography in the Caribbean classroom. *Caribbean Geography, 9*(1), 58-60.

Becken, S., Mahon, R., Rennie, H. G., & Shakeela, A. (2014). The tourism disaster vulnerability framework: An application to tourism in small island destinations. *Natural Hazards*, *71*(1), 955-972.

Binkhorst, E., & Den Dekker, T. (2009). Agenda for co-creation tourism experience research. *Journal of Hospitality Marketing & Management*, *18*(2-3), 311-327.

Blain, C., Levy, S. E., & Ritchie, J. B. (2005). Destination branding: Insights and practices from destination management organizations. *Journal of travel research*, *43*(4), 328-338.

Botero, C., Anfuso, G., Williams, A. T., Zielinski, S., Da Silva, C. P., Cervantes, O., & Cabrera, J. A. (2013). Reasons for beach choice: European and Caribbean perspectives. *Journal of Coastal Research*, *65*(Sp1), 880-885.

Bramwell, B., & Lane, B. (Eds.). (2000). *Tourism collaboration and partnerships: Politics, practice and sustainability* (Vol. 2). Bristol, UK: Channel View Publications.

Brown, K-A. (2013). *Services regulation in the Caribbean: Tourism services*. Inter-American Development Bank, IDB Technical Note No. 571. Retrieved from https://publications.iadb.org/bitstream/handle/11319/6040/SERVICES%20REGULATIO N%20IN%20THE%20CARIBBEAN-CHAPTER%205-TOURISM%20SERVICES.pdf?sequence=1

Cai, L. A. (2002). Cooperative branding for rural destinations. *Annals of Tourism Research*, *29*(3), 720-742.

Camprubí, R., Guia, J., & Comas, J. (2013). The new role of tourists in destination image formation. *Current Issues in Tourism*, *16*(2), 203-209.

Caribbean Tourism Organization. (2004). *Caribbean travel.* CTO's marketing site, including links to pages for individual destination. Retrieved from http://www.caribbeantravel.com

Caribbean Tourism Organization. (2009a). *Caribbean travel.* CTO's marketing site, including

    links to pages for individual destinations. Retrieved from

    http://www.caribbeantravel.com

Caribbean Tourism Organization. (2009b). One Caribbean. Retrieved from

    http://www.onecaribbean.org. [CTO's business site]

Chamberlin, E. H. (1933). *The theory of monopolistic competition.* Cambridge, MA: Harvard

    University Press.

Chambers, D., & McIntosh, B. (2008). Using authenticity to achieve competitive advantage in

    medical tourism in the English-speaking Caribbean. *Third World Quarterly, 29*(5), 919-

    937.

Charles, D. (2013). Sustainable tourism in the Caribbean: The role of the accommodations

    sector. *International Journal of Green Economics, 7*(2), 148-161.

Chiagouris, L. (2005). Nonprofit brands come of age. *Marketing Management, 14*

    (September/October), 30-33.

Conley, J. G., Bican, P. M., & Ernst, H. (2013). Value articulation. *California Management*

    Review, 55(4), 102-120.

Connell, J., & Fara, X. (2013). Medical tourism in the Caribbean islands: A cure for economies

    in crisis. *Island Stud J, 8*(1), 115-30.

Conway, D. (1988). Conceptualizing contemporary patterns of Caribbean international mobility.

    Caribbean Geography, 2(3), 145.

Croes, R. R. (2006). A paradigm shift to a new strategy for small island economies: Embracing

    demand side economics for value enhancement and long term economic

    stability. *Tourism Management, 27*(3), 453-465.

Croes, R., Lee, S. H., & Olson, E. D. (2013). Authenticity in tourism in small island destinations: a local perspective. *Journal of Tourism and Cultural Change, 11*(1-2), 1-20.

Day, M. (2010). Challenges and prospects of differentiating destination brands: The case of the Dutch Caribbean islands. *Journal of Travel & Tourism Marketing, 27*(1),1-13.

Daye, M. (2010). Challenges and prospects of differentiating destination brands: The case of the Dutch Caribbean islands. *Journal of Travel & Tourism Marketing, 27*(1), 1-13.

de Holan, P. M., & Phillips, N. (1997). Sun, sand, and hard currency: Tourism in Cuba. *Annals of Tourism Research, 24*(4), 777-795.

De Kadt, E. (1979). Social planning for tourism in the developing countries. *Annals of Tourism Research, 6*(1), 36–48. doi:10.1016/0160-7383(79)90093-8

Della Corte, V., & Aria, M. (2016). Coopetition and sustainable competitive advantage. The case of tourist destinations. *Tourism Management, 54*, 524-540.

Dixit, A. K., & Stiglitz, J. E. (1977). Monopolistic competition and optimum product diversity. *American Economic Review, 67*(3), 297- 308.

Echtner, C. M., & Richie, J. R. B. (1993). The measurement of destination image: An empirical assessment. *Journal of Travel Research, 31*(4), 3-13.

Fiegenbaum, A., & Karnani, A. (1991). Output flexibility—A competitive advantage for small firms. *Strategic Management Journal, 12*(2), 101–114. doi:10.1002/smj.4250120203

Fox, J. A. & Brown, L. D. (1998). *The struggle for accountability: The World Bank, NGOs, and grassroots movements*. MIT press.

Frohlick, S. (2013). Intimate tourism markets: Money, gender, and the complexity of erotic exchange in a Costa Rican Caribbean town. *Anthropological Quarterly, 86*(1), 133-162.

Galani-Moutafi, V. (2000). The self and the other: Traveler, ethnographer, tourist. *Annals of Tourism Research, 27*(1), 203-224.

Gartner, W. C. (1996). *Tourism development, principles, processes and policies.* New York, NY: Van Norstrand Reinhold.

George, B. P., & George, B. P. (2004). Past visits and the intention to revisit a destination: Place attachment as the mediator and novelty seeking as the moderator. *Journal of Tourism Studies, 15*(2), 51-69.

George, B. P., Inbakaran, R., & Poyyamoli, G. (2010). To travel or not to travel: Towards understanding the theory of nativistic motivation. *Turizam: znanstveno-stručni časopis, 58*(4), 395-407.

George, B. P., Henthorne, T. L., and Williams, A. J. (2016). Attraction diversity index: the concept, measure, and its relation with tourism destination competitiveness. *Revista Turismo, 7*(1), Forthcoming.

Gmelch, G. (2012). *Behind the smile: The working lives of Caribbean tourism.* Bloomington, IN: Indiana University Press.

Golding, J. M., & MacLeod, C. M. (2013). *Intentional forgetting: Interdisciplinary approaches.* Abingdon, UK: Psychology Press.

Grant, R. M., Jammine, A. P., & Thomas, H. (1988). Diversity, diversification, and profitability among British manufacturing companies, 1972–1984. *Academy of management Journal, 31*(4), 771-801.

Granvorka, C., & Strobl, E. (2013). The impact of hurricane strikes on tourist arrivals in the Caribbean. *Tourism Economics, 19*(6), 1401-1409.

Griffin, L. (2016). Trouble in Paradise: The Treadmill of Production and Caribbean Tourism. *Capitalism Nature Socialism, 27*(2), 83-99.

Guest, G. (2013). Describing mixed methods research: An alternative to typologies. *Journal of Mixed Methods Research, 7*(2), 141-151.

Guilamo-Ramos, V., Jaccard, J., McCarthy, K., Quiñones, Z., Lushin, V., Skinner-Day, M., ... & Meisterlin, L. (2013). Taxonomy of Caribbean tourism alcohol venues: Implications for HIV transmission. *Drug and Alcohol Dependence, 132*(1), 238-243.

Hamzah, A., & Hampton, M. P. (2013). Resilience and non-linear change in island tourism. *Tourism Geographies, 15*(1), 43-67.

Henthorne, T. L., & George, B. P. (2009). Transformation of tourism business in the communist Cuba: A critical analysis. *International Journal of Business Insights & Transformation, 3*(1), 6-13.

Henthorne, T. L., & Miller, M. M. (2003). Cuban tourism in the Caribbean context: A regional impact assessment. *Journal of Travel Research, 42*(1), 84-93.

Henthorne, T. L., George, B. P., & Smith, W. C. (2013). Risk perception and buying behavior: An examination of some relationships in the context of cruise tourism in Jamaica. *International Journal of Hospitality & Tourism Administration, 14*(1), 66-86.

Henthorne, T. L., George, B. P., and Miller, M. M. (2016). Unique selling propositions and destination branding: A longitudinal perspective on the Caribbean tourism in transition. *Tourism: An international Interdisciplinary Journal, 64*(3), forthcoming.

Herbert, B., & Christian, C. S. (2014). Regional tourism at the cross-roads: Perspectives of Caribbean tourism organization's stakeholders. *Journal of Sustainable Development, 7*(1), 17-21.

Hill, N. S., & Lewis, A. (2015). An assessment of the Caribbean tourism organization's collaborative marketing efforts: A member nation perspective. *Journal of Vacation Marketing, 21*(1), 75–85. doi:10.1177/1356766714544234

Hill, N. S., & Lewis, A. (2015). An assessment of the Caribbean tourism organization's collaborative marketing efforts A member nation perspective. *Journal of Vacation Marketing, 21*(1), 75-85.

Hingtgen, N., Kline, C., Fernandes, L., & McGehee, N. G. (2015). Cuba in transition: Tourism industry perceptions of entrepreneurial change. *Tourism Management*, 50(October), 184-193.

Hirschman, A.O. (1964). The paternity of an index. *The American Economic Review*, 54 (5), 761-762.

Hodge, G. D., & Little, W. E. (2014). Introduction: Tourism development and the policing of urban space in Latin American and the Caribbean. *The Journal of Latin American and Caribbean Anthropology, 19*(3), 389-395.

Holladay, P. J., & Powell, R. B. (2013). Resident perceptions of social–ecological resilience and the sustainability of community-based tourism development in the Commonwealth of Dominica. *Journal of Sustainable Tourism, 21*(8), 1188-1211.

Hotelling, H. (1929). Stability in Competition. *The Economic Journal, 39*(153), 41-57.

Huang, Y. C., Backman, K. F., Backman, S. J., & Chang, L. L. (2016). Exploring the Implications of Virtual Reality Technology in Tourism Marketing: An Integrated Research Framework. *International Journal of Tourism Research, 18*(2), 116-128.

Jacquemin, A. P., & Berry, C. H. (1979). Entropy measure of diversification and corporate growth. *Journal of Industrial Economics, 27*(4), 359–369.

Johnson, K. R., & Bartlett, K. R. (2013). The role of tourism in national human resource development: A Jamaican perspective. *Human Resource Development International, 16*(2), 205-219.

Jordan, L. A., & Jolliffe, L. (2013). Heritage tourism in the Caribbean: Current themes and challenges. *Journal of Heritage Tourism, 8*(1), 1-8.

JTB (2015). *Jamaican Tourism Board Statistics*. Last accessed from http://www.jtbonline.org/ on 31 December 2015.

Karagiannis, N., & Madjd-Sadjadi, Z. (2012). Crime, criminal activity and tourism performance: issues from the Caribbean. *Worldwide Hospitality and Tourism Themes, 4*(1), 73-90.

Kerstetter, D. L., & Bricker, K. S. (2012). Relationship between carrying capacity of small island tourism destinations and quality-of-life. In *Handbook of Tourism and Quality-of-Life Research* (pp. 445-462). The Netherlands: Springer.

Kramer, A. M. (2013). *Climate change adaptation and tourism in the Mexican Caribbean* (Doctoral dissertation, University of Oxford. Oxford,UK: Oxford Univeristy Press). Retrieved from http://www.envia.bl.uk/bitstream/request?itempage=handle/123456789/3373&path=http%3A%2F%2Fethos.bl.uk%2FOrderDetails.do%3Fuin%3Duk.bl.ethos.567728

Kwoka Jr, J. E. (1985). Herfindahl Index in Theory and Practice, The. *Antitrust Bull., 30*, 915.

Laframboise, N., Mwase, N., Park, J., & Zhou, Y. (2014). *Revisiting Tourism Flows to the Caribbean: What is Driving Arrivals?*. Working Paper No. 14-229. International Monetary Fund, 2014. Retrieved from https://www.imf.org/external/pubs/cat/longres.aspx?sk=42541.0

Laskey, H. A., Fox, R. J., & Crask, M. R. (1995). The relationship between advertising message strategy and television commercial effectiveness. *Journal of Advertising Research, 35* (2), 31-39.

Lee, G., Cai, L. A., & O'Leary, J. T. (2005). WWW.branding.states.US: An analysis of brand-building elements in the US state tourism websites. *Tourism Management, 27*(5), 815-828.

Lee, S., & Ramdeen, C. (2013). Cruise ship itineraries and occupancy rates. *Tourism Management, 34*(February), 236-237.

Leiper, N. (1990). Tourist attraction systems. *Annals of tourism research,17*(3), 367-384.

Lenik, S. (2013). Community engagement and heritage tourism at Geneva Estate, Dominica. *Journal of Heritage Tourism, 8*(1), 9-19.

Lerner A. P., & Singer H. W. (1937). Some Notes on Duopoly and Spatial Competition. *The Journal of Political Economy, 45*(2),145-186.

Lew, A. A. (1987). A framework of tourist attraction research. *Annals of tourism research, 14*(4), 553-575.

Lewis, V., & Winkler, R. (2015). Product Diversity, Demand Structures, And Optimal Taxation. *Economic Inquiry, 53*(2), 979-1003.

Linning, R. (2004). Abuse and self-abuse –PR and its USP: Plausible deniability. *Journal of Communication Management, 9*(1), 59-62.

Matsumoto, A., Merlone, U., & Szidarovszky, F. (2012). Some notes on applying the Herfindahl–Hirschman Index. *Applied Economics Letters, 19*(2), 181-184.

McElroy, J. L., & De Albuquerque, K. (1998). Tourism penetration index in small Caribbean islands. *Annals of Tourism Research, 25*(1), 145-168.

Meade, J. E. (1974). The optimal balance between economies of scale and variety of products: An illustrative model. *Economica,* New Series, *41*(164, November), 359-367.

Miller, M. M., & Henthorne, T. L. (2006). In search of competitive advantage in Caribbean tourism websites: Revisiting the unique selling proposition. *Journal of Travel & Tourism Marketing, 21*(2/3), 49-62.

Mintz, S. W. (1983). Caribbean marketplaces and Caribbean history. *Radical History Review,* (27), 110-120. doi:10.1215/01636545-1983-27-110

Montgomery, C. A. (1985). Product-Market Diversification and Market Power. *Academy of Management Journal, 28*(4), 789–798. doi:10.2307/256237

Moore, A. (2015). Islands of difference: design, urbanism, and sustainable tourism in the Anthropocene Caribbean. *The Journal of Latin American and Caribbean Anthropology, 20*(3), 513-532.

Morgan, N., Pritchard, A., & Pride, R. (2004). *Destination branding: Creating the unique destination proposition.* Oxford, UK: Butterworth-Heinemann.

Mosedale, J. (2006). Tourism commodity chains: market entry and its effects on St Lucia. *Current Issues in Tourism, 9*(4-5), 436-458.

Murphy, L., Benckendorff, P., & Moscardo, G. (2007). Linking travel motivation, tourist self-image and destination brand personality. *Journal of Travel & Tourism Marketing, 22*(2), 45-59.

Okumus, F., Kock, G., Scantlebury, M. M., & Okumus, B. (2013). Using local cuisines when promoting small Caribbean island destinations. *Journal of Travel & Tourism Marketing, 30*(4), 410-429.

Onafowora, O. A., & Owoye, O. (2012). Modelling international tourism demand for the Caribbean. *Tourism Economics, 18*(1), 159-180.

O'Reilly, M., & Parker, N. (2012). Unsatisfactory saturation: A critical exploration of the notion of saturated sample sizes in qualitative research. *Qualitative Research, 15*(8), 37-42. 1468794112446106.

Parasuraman, A., Zeithaml, V. A., & Berry, L. L. (1994). Reassessment of expectations as a comparison standard in measuring service quality: Implications for further research. *The Journal of Marketing, 56*(1), 111-124.

Parry, J. H., Sherlock, P. M., & Maingot, A. P. (1987). *A short history of the West Indies*. (4th ed). London, UK: Macmillan Caribbean.

Peirce, S., & Ritchie, B. W. (2007). National capital branding: A comparative case study of Canberra, Australia and Wellington, New Zealand. *Journal of Travel & Tourism Marketing, 22*(3/4), 67-78.

Pinnock, F. (2014). The future of tourism in an emerging economy: the reality of the cruise industry in Caribbean. *Worldwide Hospitality and Tourism Themes, 6*(2), 127-137.

Pitts, R. A., & Hopkins, H. D. (1982). Firm diversity: Conceptualization and measurement. *Academy of management Review, 7*(4), 620-629.

Plog, S. C. (2004). *Leisure travel*. Upper Saddle River, NJ: Prentice-Hall.

Poon, A. (1988). Innovation and the future of Caribbean tourism. *Tourism Management, 9*(3), 213-220.

Poon, A. (1990). Flexible specialization and small size: The case of Caribbean tourism. *World Development, 18*(1), 109-123.

Porter, M.E. (1990). *The competitive advantage of nations*. New York, NY: Free Press.

Pratt, S. (2015). The economic impact of tourism in SIDS. *Annals of Tourism Research, 52*(May), 148-160.

Prebensen, N. (2007). Exploring tourists' images of a distant destination. *Tourism Management, 28(*3), 747-756.

Ranaivoson, H. (2005). *The economic analysis of product diversity.* Retrieved from https://halshs.archives-ouvertes.fr/halshs-00197137/document

Reeves, R. (1961). *Reality in advertisi*ng. New York, NY: Knopf.

Richard, O. C., & Charles, C. D. (2013). Considering diversity as a source of competitive advantage in organizations. *The Oxford handbook of diversity and work*, 239-249.

Richardson, J., & Cohen, J. (1993). State slogans: The case of the missing USP. *Journal of Travel & Tourism Marketing, 2(*2 /3), 91-109.

Ridderstaat, J., & Croes, R. (2015). The Link between Money Supply and Tourism Demand Cycles. A Case Study of Two Caribbean Destinations. *Journal of Travel Research, 26*(2), 37-40.

Rihova, I., Buhalis, D., Moital, M., & Gouthro, M. B. (2015). Conceptualising customer-to-customer value co-creation in tourism. *International Journal of Tourism Research, 17*(4), 356-363.

Roberts, S., Telesford, J. N., & Barrow, J. V. (2016). Navigating the Caribbean Archipelago: An examination of regional transportation issues. In G. Baldacchino (Ed.), *Archipelago Tourism: Policies and Practices*, p. 147.

Rommen, T., & Neely, D. T. (Eds.). (2014). *Sun, sea, and sound: music and tourism in the circum-Caribbean*. Oxford, UK: Oxford University Press.

Rowley, J. (2004). Online branding. *Online Information Review, 28*(2), 131-138.

Rumelt, R. P. (1974). *Strategy, structure, and economic performance*. Boston, MA: Harvard Business School Press.

Rumelt, R. P. (1982). Diversification strategy and profitability. *Strategic Management Journal, 3*(4), 359–369. doi: 10.1002/smj.4250030407

Scott, D., Simpson, M. C., & Sim, R. (2012). The vulnerability of Caribbean coastal tourism to scenarios of climate change related sea level rise. *Journal of Sustainable Tourism, 20*(6), 883-898.

Seidl, A., Pratt, L., Honey, M., Durham, W. H., Slean, G., & Bien, A. (2014). Cruising for a bruising: Challenges in sustainable capture of ecosystem service values from cruise ship tourism in Belize. In P.A.L.D. Nunes & T. Dedeurwaerdere (Eds.), *Handbook on the Economics of Ecosystem Services and Biodiversity*, p. 40-60.

Shanka, T. (2001). Tourist destination slogans as unique selling propositions: the case of African tourism. *Tourism Analysis, 6*(1), 53-60.

Shao, A. T., & Bao, Y. (2015). Unique positioning to an elusive market: Targeting teenagers. In M. Moore & R. S. Moore, New Meanings for Marketing in a New Millennium: *Proceedings of the 2001 Academy of Marketing Science (AMS) Annual Conference* (pp. 111-117). Switzerland: Springer International Publishing. ISBN: 978-3-319-11926-7

Shaw, G. (2014). Tourism networks, knowledge dynamics and co-creation. *Knowledge Networks and Tourism, 45*, 27-31.

Sinclair-Maragh, G., & Gursoy, D. (2015). Imperialism and tourism: The case of developing island countries. *Annals of Tourism Research, 50*(January), 143-158.

Skelton, T. (2014). *Introduction to the Pan-Caribbean*. Florence, KY: Routledge.

Skipper, T. L., Carmichael, B. A., & Doherty, S. (2014). Tourism harassment experiences in Jamaica. *In* Sharpley, R., & Stone (Eds). *Contemporary tourist experience: Concepts and consequences*, pp. *27-35*. London, UK: Routledge.

Stirling, A. (1998). *On the Economics and Analysis of Diversity.* SPRU Electronic Working Paper Series No. 28. Science Policy Research Unit, Falmer, Brighton: UK. Retrieved from https://www.sussex.ac.uk/webteam/gateway/file.php?name=sewp28&site=25

Strobl, A., & Peters, M. (2013). Entrepreneurial reputation in destination networks. *Annals of Tourism Research, 40*(January), 59-82.

Tallman, S., & Li, J. (1996). Effects of international diversity and product diversity on the performance of multinational firms. *Academy of Management journal, 39*(1), 179-196.

Timms, B. F., & Conway, D. (2012). Slow tourism at the Caribbean's geographical margins. *Tourism Geographies, 14*(3), 396-418.

van der Zee, E., & Vanneste, D. (2015). Tourism networks unraveled; A review of the literature on networks in tourism management studies. *Tourism Management Perspectives, 15*(July), 46-56.

Varadarajan, P. R. (1986). Product diversity and firm performance: An empirical investigation. *The Journal of Marketing, 50*(3)43-57. American Marketing Association.

Varadarajan, P. R., & Ramanujam, V. (1987). Diversification and performance: A reexamination using a new two-dimensional conceptualization of diversity in firms. *Academy of Management Journal, 30*(2), 380-393.

Wan, W. P., & Hoskisson, R. E. (2003). Home country environments, corporate diversification strategies, and firm performance. *Academy of Management Journal, 46*(1), 27-45. doi:10.2307/30040674

Warnaby, G., & Medway, D. (2013). What about the 'place'in place marketing? *Marketing Theory*, *13*(3), 345-363.

Warner, C. (2004). Advertising. In C. Warner & J. Buchman (Eds). *Media selling: Broadcast, cable, print and interactive.* Ames, IA: Iowa State Press.

Weaver, D. B. (1998). Peripheries of the periphery: Tourism in Tobago and Barbuda. *Annals of Tourism Research, 25*(2), 292-313.

Weidenfeld, A. (2013). Tourism and cross border regional innovation systems. *Annals of Tourism Research*, *42*(July), 191-213.

Weiermair, K., & Peters, M. (2000). Tourist attractions and attracted tourists: how to satisfy today's' fickle'tourist clientele?. *Journal of Tourism Studies*, *11*(1), 22.

Weiler, L., & Dehoorne, O. (2014). Ecotourism as an Alternative to 'Sun, Sand, and Sea'Tourism Development in the Caribbean: A Comparison of Martinique and Dominica. In B-Y. Cao, S-Q, Ma, & H-h. Cao (Eds.). Ecosystem Assessment and Fuzzy Systems Management (pp. 461-469). Switzerland: Springer International Publishing.

Wilson, S., Sagewan-Alli, I., & Calatayud, A. (2014). *The ecotourism industry in the Caribbean: A value chain analysis,* No. IDB-TN-710. Inter-American Development Bank. Retrieved from https://publications.iadb.org/bitstream/handle/11319/6669/CMF_TN_Ecotourism_Industry_in_the_Caribbean.pdf

Wong, A. (2015). Caribbean Island tourism: Pathway to continued colonial servitude. *Études caribéennes*, (31-32), 8-10.

Wrigley, L. (1970). *Divisional autonomy and diversification.* Unpublished doctoral dissertation, Harvard Business School, Boston, MA.

Yilmaz, K. (2013). Comparison of quantitative and qualitative research traditions: Epistemological, theoretical, and methodological differences. *European Journal of Education, 48*(2), 311-325.

Appendices

Appendix 1

Island Nations and their USPs: A Longitudinal Comparison

Destination	USP	2004 USP and Level				
		Expert 1	Expert 2	Expert 3	USP Level	Tourist Arrivals
Anguilla	Feeling is Believing	1	2	2	2	53,987
Antigua & Barbuda	The Caribbean you've always imagined	2	2	3	2	245,797
Aruba	Where happiness lives	2	2	3	2	728,157
Bahamas	The Islands of Bahamas	0	0	0	0	1,561,312
Barbados	Just beyond your imagination	2	1	2	2	551,502
Belize	Mother Nature's Best Kept Secret	3a	3b	4a	3b	230,832
Bermuda	Out of the Blue	2	2	1	2	271,617
Bonaire	Divers Paradise	3b	2	3b	3b	63,156
British Virgin Islands	Nature's Little Secret – over 60 Caribbean	3b	3a	4a	3b	304,518
Cayman Islands	Close to Home. Far from Expected.	3b	3b	3b	3b	259,929
Cuba	(No slogan)	0	0	0	0	2,048,572
Curaçao	In the Southern Caribbean. Real.	3b	3a	2	3a	223,439
Dominica	The Nature Island of the Caribbean	4b	4a	4b	4b	80,087
Dominican Republic	Experience our Caribbean	1	1	2	1	3,443,205
Grenada	The Spice of the Caribbean	3b	3a	3a	3a	133,865
Guadeloupe	Decidedly French. Undeniably Caribbean	4a	3b	4a	4a	623134*
Guyana	(Several rotating slogans with accompanying images)	3a	3a	3b	3a	121,989
Haiti	Experience Haiti: It is unique and fascinating, it has personality	2	2	2	2	108,868
Jamaica	Explore Jamaica	1	1	1	1	1,414,786
Martinique	So much MORE than just an Island	2	3a	3b	3a	470,890
Montserrat	One Hundred Thousand Welcomes	2	2	1	2	10,138
Nevis	Nevis…Naturally	2	3a	3b	3a	
Puerto Rico	The Shining Star	1	2	1	1	3,684,108
St. Barths	(No slogan)	0	0	0	0	*
St. Eustatius	The Caribbean's Hidden Treasure	3a	3b	3b	3b	11,076
St. Kitts & Nevis	Two Islands. One Paradise	1	2	1	1	91,769
St. Lucia	Simply Beautiful	3a	2	3b	3a	298,431
St. Maarten	A little European a lot Caribbean	3b	3a	3b	3b	
St. Martin	Friendly Caribbean. French Caribbean	3b	3b	3b	3b	*
St. Vincent & The Grenadines	Jewels of the Caribbean	2	3b	4a	3b	86,721
Suriname	The Beating Heart of the Amazon	4a	4b	4b	4b	102,553
Trinidad & Tobago	Come to life	1	2	1	1	442,555
Turks and Caicos Islands	The everything island	1	3a	2	3a	150,579
US Virgin Islands	America's Caribbean	4a	4b	4b	4a	658,638

*St. Barths, St. Martin included in numbers for Guadeloupe

Destination	USP	Expert 1	Expert 2	Expert 3	USP Level	Tourist Arrivals
Anguilla	Tranquility wrapped in blue	3a	3b	2	3a	57,891
Antigua & Barbuda	The beach is just the beginning	3a	3a	3b	3a	234,410
Aruba	90,000 friends you haven't met yet	2	3b	3b	3b	812,623
Bahamas	It's Better in the Bahamas	1	1	1	1	1,326,722
Barbados	Welcome to Barbados: the official	4a	3b	3b	3b	518,564
Belize	Mother Nature's Best Kept Secret	4b	4a	4b	4b	232,373
Bermuda	Feel the Love	2	2	2	2	235,860
Bonaire	Once a Visitor Always a Friend	1	2	3a	2	66,998
British Virgin Islands	Nature's Little Secrets	3a	3a	2	3a	308,793
Cayman Islands	Close to Home. Far from Expected.	3b	3b	3b	3b	271,958
Cuba	(No slogan)	0	0	0	0	2,429,809
Curaçao	The Curaçao difference	4a	2	3a	3a	366,703
Dominica	Defy the Everyday. Dominica. The	4b	4b	4b	4b	74,923
Dominican Republic	DR endless. Has it all	3a	3b	3b	3b	3,992,303
Grenada	The Spice of the Caribbean	4a	3b	4b	4a	113,370
Guadeloupe	Archipelago of Discoveries	3b	3a	3b	3b	623134*
Guyana	(A few rotating slogans with accompanying images)	3b	3b	4a	3b	141,281
Haiti	Part French, Part African, Part Caribbean – 100% Unforgettable	4a	3b	4a	4a	386,060
Jamaica	Once you go, you know	3a	3b	3a	3a	1,831,097
Martinique	Color Me Martinique	3b	3b	3b	3b	441,647
Montserrat	A Caribbean Treasure – Spectacular by Nature	3b	4a	4b	4a	6,311
Nevis	Naturally	2	3a	4a	3a	
Puerto Rico	Explore beyond the shore	3b	3a	3b	3b	3,607,752
St. Barths	The Art of Being an Island	3a	3a	2	3a	*
St. Eustatius	The Caribbean's Hidden Treasure	2	2	3b	3a	12,049
St. Kitts & Nevis	An Experience Like No Other	3a	3a	3a	3a	106,408
St. Lucia	Simply Beautiful	3a	2	3b	3a	278,491
St. Maarten	Magical St. Maarten	4a	4a	4a	4a	440,185
St. Martin	The Friendly Island	3a	3b	3a	3a	*
St. Vincent & The Grenadines	The Caribbean You're Looking for	3a	3a	2	3a	75,446
Suriname	The Beating Heart of the Amazon	4b	4b	4b	4b	150,396
Trinidad & Tobago	The True Caribbean	3b	3a	3b	3b	371,889
Turks and Caicos Islands	Beautiful by Nature	3a	3a	3a	3a	264,887
US Virgin Islands	America's Caribbean	4a	4a	4a	4a	562,300

*St. Barths, St. Martin included in numbers for Guadeloupe

| Destination | USP | 2014 USP and Level | | | | |
		Expert 1	Expert 2	Expert 3	USP Level	Tourist Arrivals (2013)
Anguilla	Tranquility wrapped in blue	3a	3a	3a	3a	69,068
Antigua & Barbuda	The beach is just the beginning	3b	3a	2	3a	243,923
Aruba	One happy island	2	2	2	2	979,256
Bahamas	(No slogan)	0	0	0	0	1,363,487
Barbados	The home of our music icon, Riahnna	4a	4b	4b	4b	508,520
Belize	Discover How To Be	3b	4a	4a	4a	294,176
Bermuda	So much more	1	2	1	1	236,343
Bonaire	Once a Visitor Always a Friend	1	2	1	1	
British Virgin Islands	Nature's Little Secrets	3a	3a	3a	3a	355,677
Cayman Islands	(No slogan)	0	0	0	0	345,387
Cuba	Autentica Cuba	3a	3a	3a	3a	2,851,330
Curaçao	(Several rotating slogans with	3a	3b	3a	3a	440,044
Dominica	The Nature Island	3b	4a	3b	3b	78,277
Dominican Republic	Has it all	2	2	2	2	4,689,770
Grenada	The Spice of the Caribbean	4a	3b	4a	4a	116,456
Guadeloupe	(No slogan)	0	0	0	0	
Guyana	South America Undiscovered	4a	4a	4a	4a	165,841
Haiti	Your Next Favorite Destination In The Caribbean	1	1	1	1	419,736
Jamaica	Now,that's what I call all right	1	2	2	2	2,008,409
Martinique	fleur des caraibes	4a	4b	4b	4b	489,706
Montserrat	(No slogan)	0	0	0	0	7,202
Nevis	Naturally	2	3a	4a	3a	
Puerto Rico	The all star island	2	1	1	1	1,588,677
St. Barths	(No slogan)	0	0	0	0	
St. Eustatius	Dutch Caribbean	4a	4b	4a	4a	
St. Kitts & Nevis	Follow your heart	2	3a	3a	3a	100,997
St. Lucia	Simply Beautiful	2	3a	3a	3a	318,626
St. Maarten	(No slogan)	0	0	0	0	467,259
St. Martin	The Friendly Island, French Caribbean.	3a	3b	3b	3b	
St. Vincent & The Grenadines	(A few rotating slogans with	3b	3b	3b	3b	71,725
Suriname	Suriname, A Colorful Experience... Exotic	2	2	2	2	249,102
Trinidad & Tobago	The True Caribbean	3a	3b	3b	3b	
Turks and Caicos Islands	Beautiful by Nature	3a	3a	3a	3a	290,587
US Virgin Islands	(No slogan)	0	0	0	0	702,963

*St. Barths, St. Martin included in numbers for Guadeloupe

Appendix 2

Caribbean Tourism Destination Management Organization Websites

Destination	Official Website
Anguilla	www.ivisitanguilla.com
Antigua & Barbuda	www.visitantiguabarbuda.com
Aruba	www.aruba.com
Bahamas	www.bahamas.com
Barbados	www.visitbarbados.org
Belize	www.travelbelize.org
Bermuda	www.gotobermuda.com
Bonaire	www.tourismbonaire.com
British Virgin Islands	www.bvitourism.com/
Cayman Islands	www.caymanislands.ky
Cuba	www.cubatravel.tur.cu
Curaçao	www.curacao.com
Dominica	www.dominica.dm/
Dominican Republic	www.godominicanrepublic.com
Grenada	www.grenadagrenadines.com/
Guadeloupe	www.lesilesdeguadeloupe.com
Guyana	www.guyana-tourism.com
Haiti	www.haititourisminc.com
Jamaica	www.visitjamaica.com
Martinique	www.martinique.org
Montserrat	www.visitmontserrat.com
Nevis	www.nevisisland.com
Puerto Rico	www.seepuertorico.com
St. Barths	www.st-barths.com
St. Eustatius	www.statiatourism.com
St. Kitts & Nevis	www.stkittstourism.kn
St. Lucia	www.stlucianow.com
St. Maarten	www.st-maarten.com
St. Martin	www.stmartinisland.org
St. Vincent & The Grenadines	www.discoversvg.com
Suriname	www.surinametourism.sr
Trinidad & Tobago	www.gotrinidadandtobago.com
Turks and Caicos Islands	www.turksandcaicostourism.com
US Virgin Islands	http://www.visitusvi.com/

Appendix 3

Attraction Diversity Index Calculation

Destination	Attraction Cluster Value i (Relative Value of Attraction Cluster 'i')						HHI	Attraction Diversity Index	ADI Level
	Beach & Beach Activities	Cultural Heritage Attractions	Wilderness Attractions	Shopping, City, and Night Life	Business Attractions	Miscellaneous Other Attractions			
Anguilla	0.36	0.19	0.05	0.32	0.07	0.01	0.2755	3.629764065	High Diversity
Antigua & Barbuda	0.39	0.32	0.1	0.1	0.03	0.06	0.2754	3.631082062	Low Diversity
Aruba	0.32	0.19	0.2	0.1	0.1	0.09	0.1985	5.037783375	Low Diversity
Bahamas	0.24	0.04	0.09	0.23	0.31	0.09	0.2163	4.623208507	Low Diversity
Barbados	0.25	0.21	0.11	0.12	0.27	0.04	0.206	4.854368932	Medium Diversity
Belize	0.28	0.11	0.31	0.14	0.08	0.08	0.2126	4.703668862	Medium Diversity
Bermuda	0.27	0.21	0.09	0.19	0.22	0.02	0.2096	4.770992366	Medium Diversity
Bonaire	0.22	0.17	0.31	0.06	0.09	0.15	0.1851	5.402485143	Medium Diversity
British Virgin Islands	0.38	0.07	0.19	0.21	0.04	0.11	0.2311	4.327131112	Medium Diversity
Cayman Islands	0.31	0.05	0.07	0.25	0.32	0.05	0.2639	3.789314134	Medium Diversity
Cuba	0.09	0.51	0.07	0.02	0.12	0.19	0.2879	3.473428274	Medium Diversity
Curaçao	0.59	0.17	0.08	0.07		0.09	0.3883	2.575328354	Low Diversity
Dominica	0.22	0.21	0.25	0.23	0.07	0.02	0.2128	4.69924812	Low Diversity
Dominican Republic	0.21	0.21	0.08	0.21	0.28	0.01	0.2171	4.606172271	Low Diversity
Grenada	0.25	0.05	0.28	0.22	0.09	0.11	0.1999	5.002501251	Medium Diversity
Guadeloupe	0.38	0.07	0.09	0.22		0.24	0.2058	4.859086492	Medium Diversity
Guyana	0.29	0.08	0.21	0.17	0.05	0.2	0.166	6.024096386	Medium Diversity
Haiti	0.21	0.22	0.19	0.02	0.02	0.34	0.1294	7.72797527	Medium Diversity
Jamaica	0.31	0.38	0.03	0.08	0.19	0.01	0.2839	3.522367031	Medium Diversity
Martinique	0.71	0.08	0.03	0.15		0.03	0.5339	1.873009927	High Diversity
Montserrat	0.48	0.19	0.07	0.11		0.15	0.2835	3.527336861	Low Diversity
Nevis	0.38	0.09	0.2	0.25		0.08	0.255	3.921568627	Low Diversity
Puerto Rico	0.19	0.26	0.11	0.17	0.21	0.06	0.1888	5.296610169	Low Diversity
St. Barths	0.25	0.02	0.06	0.2	0.41	0.06	0.2746	3.641660597	Low Diversity
St. Eustatius	0.61	0.13	0.17	0.08		0.01	0.4243	2.356823003	Medium Diversity
St. Kitts & Nevis	0.23	0.16	0.04	0.12	0.31	0.14	0.1906	5.246589717	Low Diversity
St. Lucia	0.51	0.07	0.17	0.12		0.13	0.3083	3.243593902	Low Diversity
St. Maarten	0.45	0.12	0.12	0.23		0.08	0.2842	3.518648839	Medium Diversity
St. Martin	0.51	0.13	0.21	0.12		0.03	0.3355	2.980625931	Low Diversity
St. Vincent & The Grenadines	0.32	0.33	0.11	0.02		0.22	0.2238	4.468275246	Low Diversity
Suriname	0.22	0.12	0.12	0.1	0.03	0.41	0.0881	11.3507378	Low Diversity
Trinidad & Tobago	0.19	0.18	0.19	0.11	0.31	0.02	0.2128	4.69924812	Medium Diversity
Turks and Caicos Islands	0.31	0.06	0.18	0.24	0.02	0.19	0.1901	5.260389269	High Diversity
US Virgin Islands	0.35	0.17	0.06	0.21	0.17	0.04	0.228	4.385964912	Medium Diversity

www.ingramcontent.com/pod-product-compliance
Lightning Source LLC
Chambersburg PA
CBHW070107210526
45170CB00013B/782